Scotland's Heritage

Scotland's Heritage

a pictorial journey through Scotland described by Lawrence Stenhouse

COLLINS 144 Cathedral Street Glasgow C.4

General Editor: J. B. Foreman
Executive Editor: Sandra Bance

SBN 00 411124 9

(c) 1970 William Collins Sons and Company Limited

Foreword

The fabric of a nation's heritage is not
adequately described by words or pictures.
But for the visitor to Scotland we have tried
to isolate two memorable threads in the
country's life, its beauty and its social and
political history. We follow a pictorial journey
through Scotland, setting out in the south-
west, travelling north to the Highlands and
islands and then returning south down the
eastern side. The text describes what the
traveller sees at each stage of this journey,
and fills in the historical and literary
background to his encounters.

The marriage of pictures and text in a book is
often an awkward one. In this book we have
tried to keep them in close relation with one
another, so that any place can be selected
from the index or from the illustrations, and
read as a unit on its own, the text serving as a
commentary to the pictures. But we have also
preserved a continuity so that the book can be
read as a whole, as an intinerary with
commentary, a stimulant to the tourist, or a
reviver of memories.

We hope that we have in this way produced a
book which does not attempt to dominate the
reader but is rather submissive to his mood
and responsive to his purposes.

Acknowledgments

We wish to acknowledge our debt to George Outram and Co., Ltd., proprietors of *Scottish Field*, for the use of the colour photographs in this book. The black and white photographs were kindly made available to us by the following:

Barnaby's Picture Library
David MacBraynes Ltd.
George Outram & Co. Ltd.
J. Allan Cash
Leslie Nimmo
L. P. Chappell
Ministry of Public Building and Works
National Gallery of Scotland
National Trust for Scotland
N. of Scotland Hydro-Electric Board
Scottish National Portrait Gallery
Scottish Tourist Board
Society of Antiquaries of Scotland
Upper Clyde Shipbuilders
Wm. Grant and Sons Ltd.

See index of illustrations on page 202.

The Queen of the South, Dumfries, sits astride the River Nith, having gathered to her skirts Maxwelltown, her neighbour on the western bank. For the traveller who does not rush heedlessly by car or by train northward over Beattock, this is the gateway to Scotland, a royal burgh since the twelfth century, Burns' "Maggie by the Banks o' Nith, A dame with pride eneugh"; and indeed enough to be proud of for she is a pleasant town of warm red sandstone with five fine, honest bridges and an eventful history. The name means 'fort of the copse', from the Gaelic *Dunphris*. The poet Robert Burns was an elected burgess and spent his last years in the town and on his nearby farm Ellisland. Two local taverns house relics of his broken life. He died here and is buried in the churchyard.

The Midsteeple or Old Town Hall (1704), a prominent feature of High Street.

Left, Dumfries with the 15th-century Old Bridge straddling the waters of the Nith. Now only a footbridge, it leads through Friars' Vennel to the large statue of Burns in High Street.

Loch Doon

The broad and fertile valley of Nithsdale
penetrates northwards from Dumfries, past
the fourteenth-century tower at Closeburn,
probably the oldest house in Scotland still
used for domestic residence, to the foot of
the old Roman road which strikes north-
eastward over the Dalveen Pass. The modern
road climbs north-west to Sanquhar, where
the Covenanters under the ill-fated Richard
Cameron issued the Declaration renouncing
allegiance to Charles II.

The rough, mountainous highland on
either side of the pass, north eastward towards
Tinto Hill and south westward to Loch Doon,
Loch Trool and Merrick, is Covenanting
country. In such wild parts the stout, fanatical
adherents of the national Covenant held their
hunted and forbidden conventicles in the
Killing Times, and here too when hunted and
outlawed they were driven, as Scott has it,
"to hide themselves in dens and caves of the
earth, where they had not only to struggle
with the real dangers of damp, darkness and
famine, but were called upon, in their
disordered imaginations, to oppose the infernal
powers by whom such caverns were believed
to be haunted."

Nowadays, car and railway have slackened
the grasp of such wild places upon the
imagination, and a new value has been set
upon the solitary places of this region and
their quiet beauty. South of Loch Doon the
country is as rough and lonely as any in
Scotland, its seclusion protected by a lesser
reputation than the Highlands. And in a
strange way this core of sternness and strength
lies beneath the surface of life in Dumfries
and the towns of Galloway, a hint here or
there conveyed by rod or stout boot, an
endurance in the character of the people.

Eastward from Dumfries by contrast there unrolls the carpet of softer and more fertile country, which runs down to the English border and Carlisle. It is a countryside of border relics, some of conflict and some of peaceful contact.

Scots Dyke, an old ditch and embankment running from the Esk to the Sark, was a sixteenth-century attempt to define a debatable and now superseded frontier. Originally, it bore the royal arms of England on one side and of Scotland on the other, the early equivalents of the two roadsigns which welcome the modern traveller, whether bound north or south across Sark Bridge. But the name which really convinces the motorist that he is now in Scotland is Gretna Green, the first village, and consequently the destination for many years of runaway couples seeking the easy marriage which Scots law, abhorrent of bastardy, offered even to the visitor. Until 1856 a wedding could be achieved simply by a declaration before witnesses, and though since that date twenty-one days' residence in Scotland and the presence of a minister or registrar have been required, minors may still marry without parental consent.

Immediately north up the main road lies the village and parish of Kirkpatrick-Fleming near which is a neolithic cave, a more famous place of refuge than those of the Covenanters if legend be right in locating here Bruce's famous encounter with the spider.

Yet another border legend is commemorated in the nearby churchyard of Kirkconnell. Here are the graves of Fair Helen and her lover, Adam Fleming. When her official suitor, Bell of Middlebie, came to their meeting-place intent on murdering his rival, Helen interposed herself and was killed by the shot intended for Adam. He murdered Bell in turn and escaped abroad to mourn:

I wish my grave were growing green,
A winding-sheet drawn owre my e'en,
And I in Helen's arms lying,
On fair Kirkconnell lea.

A wish time has granted!

The Old Toll Bar, Gretna Green, the first house in Scotland and a popular spot for a wedding ceremony over the anvil.

Northwards again lies the trim village of Ecclefechan where the great historian and man of letters, Thomas Carlyle, was born. His birthplace, "The Arched House", was well built by his father and uncle, both of whom were stone masons. Carlyle was buried in the local churchyard, which contains also the grave of a lesser but intriguing local worthy, Archibald Arnott, who was doctor to Napoleon during his confinement on St. Helena.

This is a district of powerful families as well as of literature and lovers. Even the most powerful King of Scotland could not afford lightly to weaken those of his nobles who manned this border, lest by doing so he should lose his bulwark against the neighbouring English.

The great family of de Brus, proud and noble enough to intermarry with royalty and thus provide Robert the Bruce with his claim to the throne, hails from these parts. The Bruces were lords of Annandale and the castle at Annan was originally their main seat, though in the thirteenth century they greatly developed their castle at Lochmaben, a town dominated by the English for most of the fourteenth century.

At its last siege in 1588, Lochmaben Castle was defended by a Maxwell, a member of another great border family dominant in the district, whose seat was the castle of Caerlaverock, an impressive triangular castle built at the close of the thirteenth century and elaborated by successive lords until in 1640 it was captured and partly dismantled by the Covenanting forces. Its impressive Renaissance facade still hints at a history of power and intrigue stretching back to the sixth century and probably earlier.

Annan, once accesible to sailing ships from the Solway Firth, but now reliant upon agriculture.

Caerlaverock Castle.

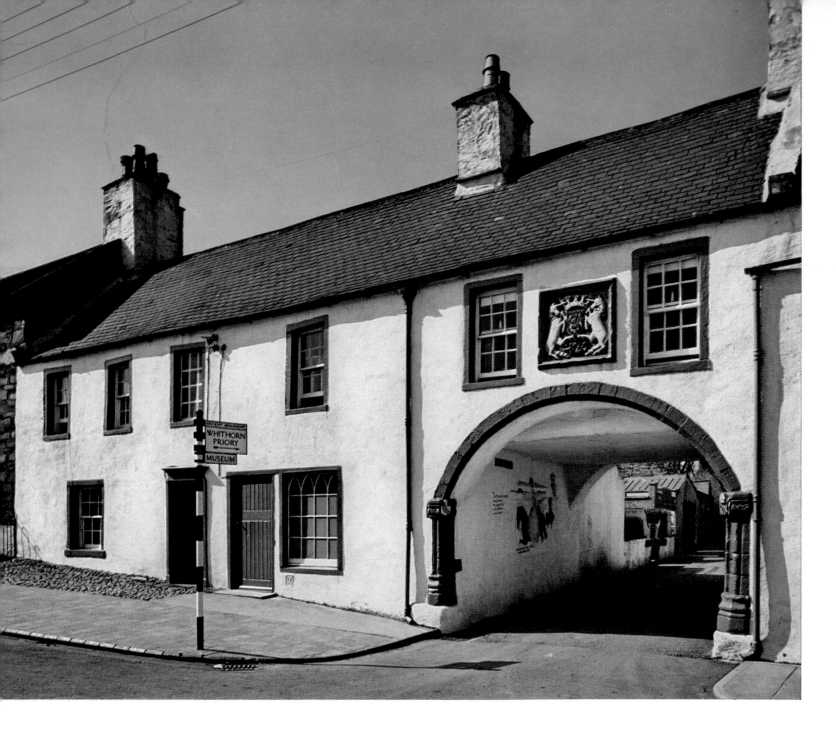

Whithorn Priory, a 4th century foundation visited by Robert Bruce, James IV and Mary Queen of Scots.

The South-West contains in miniature much of the religious history of Scotland. If the Covenanters left tales and tombstones, the Church left more durable and less stern monuments. One of the oldest comes from the village of Ruthwell, which boasts one of the great Dark Age Christian relics of Europe, the eighteen-foot carved stone Ruthwell Cross. Inscribed on it is a quotation in runic characters from the ancient mystic poem, *The Dream of the Rood* (*Cross*).

Whithorn, to the west, is one of the oldest Christian centres in Britain. Here, reputedly in A.D. 397, St. Ninian built the first stone church in Scotland, and founded the famous Candida Casa or White House, the monastery which was the basis of his missionary work.

In addition to the Whithorn monuments, there are remains of three Cistercian houses nearby.

Glenluce Abbey in Wigtownshire is largely ruined, though a fine late fifteenth-century chapter house has survived almost intact as well as an interesting water supply system. Dundrennan Abbey in Kirkcudbrightshire is an impressive ruin, set in wooded land in a quiet valley close by a stream.

The most substantial survival is New Abbey, also in Kirkcudbrightshire. This was founded in 1273, the last pre-Reformation Cistercian house in Scotland, and was colonized from Dundrennan. It was endowed by Devorgilla, Lady of Galloway, who was buried in front of the high altar in 1289 together with the embalmed heart of her husband, John Balliol of Barnard Castle.

New Abbey, Kirkcudbrightshire, often called 'Sweetheart Abbey' after Devorgilla's 'sweet silent companion', her husband's heart.

13

Castle Douglas, seen across Carlingwark Loch whose marl used to be dredged and sold as fertiliser.

Galloway, lying to the west of Dumfries, comprises both the county of Wigtown and the Stewartry of Kirkcudbright, so called because when the Balliols were stripped of their lordship, Kirkcudbright was placed under a royal stewardship, for long a hereditary office of the Maxwells.

This is a pleasant stretch of country with an attractive coastline, which draws not only holiday-makers but traditionally too, a colony of artists. There are also many local literary associations, not only with Scott and S. R. Crockett, but also with more recent authors. The greater part of the action in John Buchan's *Thirty-Nine Steps* takes place here, and the plot of Dorothy L. Sayers' *Five Red Herrings* is closely woven into the local topography.

Castle Douglas, the market and commercial centre of the Stewartry, is a thriving town well set on Carlingwark Loch, along whose shore it has developed an attractive park. The governmental capital is Kirkcudbright, an ancient royal burgh on the Dee estuary. As well as the ruined sixteenth-century castle and the seventeenth-century tolbooth, the town contains several virtually intact eighteenth-century streets and that peaceful remembrance of past bustle and trading prosperity, a once-busy harbour. One of Scotland's better-known artists, E. A. Hornel, lived here, and there is a Hornel Museum with a good collection of his paintings as well as the Stewartry Museum which houses local antiquities of the county. Gatehouse of Fleet, the "Kippletringan" of Scott's *Guy Mannering*, is another quiet town in the local style. Most of the Kirkcudbright towns were shaped by the prosperity of small industries or now-vanished coastal shipping and have been preserved from decay by the wealthy farming hinterland and their power to attract tourists and retired people.

Gatehouse of Fleet, showing the Murray Arms where Burns wrote "Scots Wha Hae", and the exotic clocktower.

Wigtown, the county town of the neighbouring shire, is in the same spirit, a quiet little place sitting on a harbour in decline. A more violent past is recorded in the churchyard, where five Covenanting martyrs are buried, among them the famous "Wigtown Martyrs", Margaret Lachlan, a woman of 63, and Margaret Wilson, a girl of 18, who, it is said, were tied to a stake on the foreshore at the river mouth and left to drown as the tide came in.

The western seaboard of Wigtownshire terminates in the Rinns of Galloway, the double peninsula with the dramatic quality of an island, which Scotland stretches out towards Ireland. The prow of the Rinns is the Mull of Galloway, a precipitous headland marked by a famous light. This is the southernmost point in Scotland, only 26 miles from the coast of Ireland and less than 23 miles from the Isle of Man.

The Rinns of Galloway has always been an isolated district, tenacious of old customs, and yet through it has always run one of the main routes to Ireland. The original sea route was from the aptly-named Portpatrick, but the danger of severe gales on the exposed outer coast was always a disadvantage and the harbour has now fallen into disuse and silted up, leaving the town to develop as a holiday centre. The trade and traffic have moved to Stranraer, the longer voyage being amply compensated by the shelter of Loch Ryan. From here the motor-ferry sails regularly to Larne. Stranraer itself is a crowded town with an appealing older section, and serves as a centre for farmers and tourists as well as a port.

Portpatrick, once an important commercial harbour, but battered to extinction by the seas and slowly choked by silting.

Girvan harbour, approximately half way from Ballantrae to Ayr.

North of the Rinns, the road which runs up the coast from Ballantrae is one of the finest coast roads in Britain. It was over a cliff on this coast that, according to the ballad, the baron of Carleton Castle disposed of seven wives before his eighth, May Cullean, consigned him to the same fate.

Girvan is a holiday resort with a small fishing fleet, a harbour which is once again crowded since the modern fashion for sailing, and a high reputation for golf and sea-trout fishing. Off its harbour lies the stark and lonely island of Ailsa Craig, "Paddy's Milestone", marking the half-way point on the sea voyage from Glasgow to Belfast. The name Ailsa Craig has been appropriated for a number of strains of vegetables first developed in this fertile county of Ayrshire.

Just to the north on the way to Ayr is one of the great masterpieces of the celebrated architect Robert Adam, the superbly elegant Culzean Castle, built in the 1780's for the Earl of Cassillis. Here there was a suite reserved for the use of the American General Eisenhower as a gesture in recognition of his leadership of the allied invasion of Europe during the Second World War.

Ayr itself, celebrated by Burns as:

Auld Ayr, wham ne'er a town surpasses,
For honest men and bonnie lasses,

dates from the early thirteenth century. Rich in historical monuments and memories of Burns, the town is one of the handsomest and busiest in the area. Its splendid shore attracts holiday-makers all summer, and the crowds are swelled by golfers and visitors to Ayr races.

The County Buildings of Ayr, a city whose charter dates from the 13th century.

B

The harbour at Brodick, Isle of Arran, showing Goat Fell (2,866 ft.) in the distance.

Close to Ayr is another seaside holiday resort which has become Scotland's most modern international gateway. Prestwick airport, recently provided with spacious modern buildings, is both an international terminal and a staging post for transatlantic airlines bound onwards to London, Amsterdam or Copenhagen.

The planes swoop in over the Isle of Arran, which lies across the entrance to the Firth of Clyde. Arran is the most accessible of the islands of the west coast and is a favourite holiday resort. Here in small compass is untamed mountainous scenery, a reflection of what lies to the north. Brodick, Lamlash and Whiting Bay, together with innumerable cottages, cater for the annual influx of holidaymakers, some who seek company on the shore, others who turn to the hills for the solitude of which a modern poet who grew up here, Alastair Reid, has written:

> *. . . a quiet quilt of heather where bees slept,*
> *and a single slow bird in circles winding*
> *round the axis of my head.*

The other islands which with Arran go to make up the county of Bute lie north within the Firth of Clyde. The Great Cumbrae and Little Cumbrae are small islands, the one almost four miles long by two miles broad and the other two miles by one mile. Apart from Millport on Great Cumbrae, the main interest is in the scenery and in the unique Scottish Marine Biological Station at Keppel. The remaining island of the shire, Bute, is above all others the resort "doon the watter" for the industrial west of Scotland. Rothesay's historic past has been overshadowed by its fame as *the* Scottish holiday resort, combining seaside attractions with a quiet hinterland and views of the mainland mountains.

Centre, a view across Rothesay Bay, with Port Bannatyne in the far distance.

Left, Rothesay Castle. The four round towers date from the 13th century, the north entrance (shown here) being added by James V in the early 16th century.

It is the industrial towns of North Ayrshire, Renfrewshire and Lanarkshire which feed the holiday resorts—Kilmarnock with its whisky, carpets, shoes and agricultural machinery, Ardeer with its huge explosives factory, Beith with its cabinet-making.

The towns on the Clyde estuary, Greenock, Dumbarton and Clydebank, are world famous for shipbuilding and all its related industries, rope and sail-making and instrument manufacture, for example. This has been one of the great shipbuilding centres of the world, and many famous ships have been built here from the early *Comet* and the golden-age Clyde railway steamers to the *Lusitania* and the Cunard Queens.

Paisley, which is the administrative centre of the county of Renfrewshire, grew originally from a settlement round the twelfth-century abbey, which preceded the present mid-fifteenth-century building, but it is interesting in modern times rather for its industrial than for its ecclesiastical history. It has long been a centre of the Scottish textile industry, famous for both cotton and silk. Paisley shawls and Paisley patterns are famous and modern Paisley is noted as one of the world's greatest thread spinning centres. There are also survivals of the west of Scotland tobacco industry as well as modern engineering works.

Eastward lies the county of Lanarkshire, again rich in monuments of industrial history. Of particular interest is New Lanark, founded in 1783 by the philanthropist, David Dale, as a model cotton-spinning centre, and famous for the managerial, social and educational experiments of Dale's son-in-law, Robert Owen. The great Lanarkshire coalfield is now contracting as pits close, though the steel works, "furnaces set on the dark plain like gigantic chessmen", are carrying on from the golden age of shipbuilding to that of motor-cars and refrigerators.

Above, Greenock, on the Firth of Clyde, birthplace of James Watt, now famous for its shipyards. Below, Paisley Abbey, showing the St. Mirin Chapel (1498) connected to the south transept. To the right is the Town Hall.

The Glasgow Docks, key to the heart of the city's trading wealth, since the great tobacco lords of the 19th century.

Of all this industrial region Glasgow is the natural centre, the largest of Scotland's cities, a great port and mart and in itself important for its factories and industry.

Glasgow is probably a more ancient city than Edinburgh, dating back to a sixth-century settlement on a strategically placed ford on the River Clyde, which was associated with Glasgow's patron saint, St. Kentigern,

familiarly known as St. Mungo. In the sixteenth and seventeenth centuries this was a small episcopal city, much praised for its pleasant beauty. It was not until the trading potential of America began to be developed from the end of the seventeenth century that Glasgow's situation on a westward-facing river began to establish the city as a trading centre, especially at first for tobacco.

The revolt of the American colonies in 1775 killed the tobacco trade, and Glasgow turned to cotton, sharing the primacy in Europe with Lancashire. Then, the invention and development of the steam engine opened the way for prosperity based on steel and engineering and shipbuilding as well as trade. The nineteenth century proved a period of expansion, and since Glasgow, like most Scottish cities, was built in enduring stone, it remains largely Victorian in character.

Glasgow's position on the river did not merely provide her with trade and a site for shipbuilding: it also made her accessible to immigrants and she has drawn many of her citizens from Ireland and from the highlands of Scotland. The Glasgow character is compounded of this mixture.

George Square, Glasgow, its Christmas decorations surveyed from his pedestal by Sir Walter Scott.

21

Necropolis. It was opened in 1832 on a rocky knoll which makes an impressive site, and Glasgow merchants vied with one another in death as in life by erecting elaborate tombs evocative of the architectural styles of every place in the world which Glaswegians visited for trade or pleasure.

All that remains of the once much-admired Glasgow Cross are two steeples, the Tron, built in 1637, which survived when St. Mary's Church was burnt in 1793, and the Tolbooth steeple which dates from 1626. The Mercat Cross is a twentieth-century copy.

Immediately to the west of the High Street lies the newer part of the city which contains the main shopping streets, Argyle Street, Buchanan Street and Sauchiehall Street, and the business and commercial quarter. In George Square are the City Chambers, a heavy exercise in Italian Renaissance style, and close by looms the contrasting Livingstone Tower of the University of Strathclyde, formerly the Royal College of Science and Technology, successor to Anderson's College, where David Livingstone studied medicine.

Above, Glasgow Cathedral, seen from the Necropolis. The crypt contains the shrine of St. Mungo, buried there in 603. The Royal Infirmary, dominates the north side of the building. Right, Hutcheson's Hospital, on the corner of Ingram St. and John St., built 1801-3 in memory of the Hutcheson brothers.

The old High Street of Glasgow bounds the east end of the modern city centre, running down from the cathedral to Glasgow Cross, where it intersects the Trongate and the Gallowgate.

The cathedral itself is a splendid building, mostly fifteenth-century, though parts of it are three centuries earlier. Its most spectacular features are the vaulted crypt, claimed to be the finest in Europe, and an interesting rood screen depicting the Seven Deadly Sins. Facing the cathedral across Cathedral Square is the oldest surviving house in Glasgow, Provand's Lordship, which dates from 1471. On the other side of the cathedral, less ancient but no less interesting, lies the merchants'

The other and older university lies away in the west end of the city at the extremity of Argyle Street, having moved from its original site in the High Street in 1870. It occupies a striking position on Gilmorehill overlooking the River Kelvin, and its 300-foot spire can be seen from miles outside the city boundaries. Glasgow University was founded by Papal Bull in 1451, the fourth oldest university in Great Britain, though its nineteenth-century buildings and urban vitality belie its age. It is one of the great universities of the world and many famous scholars, men of letters and figures in public life have been educated here. The university library is an important collection and the university holds also the Hunterian Museum and Library founded by the bequest of the collection of Dr. William Hunter, the famous eighteenth-century physician.

Across the River Kelvin from the university in the setting of Kelvingrove Park is the City of Glasgow Art Gallery and Museum, housed in an elaborate, red sandstone building. The museum is an interesting one with particularly strong collections of ship models, armour and engineering. The art collection is one of the greatest in Britain, including among its pictures work by Botticelli, Giorgione and Rembrandt and outstanding collections of French Impressionists and Scottish artists.

Farther up the Kelvin are the Royal Botanic Gardens opposite Broadcasting House, the Scottish headquarters of the B.B.C. They lie in the heart of the western residential district of substantial and often distinguished nineteenth-century houses. These are strung out along Great Western Road, which leads from the city to the north-west, to the natural playgrounds of the Firth of Clyde with its incomparable sailing, and on to the Western Highlands.

The Botanical Gardens. On the right is the Kibble Palace, which displays flora from all over the world.

Young Glaswegians.

Loch Lomond

Best known of all the attractions on Glasgow's doorstep is Loch Lomond, the largest and one of the most beautiful lakes in Britain. It is about twenty-four miles long. The southern part is broad and dotted with islands, and a long narrower arm reaches northward.

The largest of the islands is Inchmurrin, "isle of the spear," on which are the ruins of the old castle of the Lennox family. Inchcailloch, "island of old women", is the burial place of the MacGregors and has a ruined nunnery. Among the other descriptively named islands whose meanings we can guess at are Inchmoan, "the peat isle," Inchconnachan, "the dog isle," Inchtavannach, "the monk's isle," and Inchlonaig, "the marsh isle." The islands are rocky and wooded.

Loch Lomond has a steamer, *The Maid of the Loch*, which sails the length of the Loch from Balloch to Ardlui, crossing from bank to bank to call at Balmaha, Luss, Rowardenan, Tarbet and Inversnaid. Recently, the water has become busy with cruisers and sailing dinghies, speedboats and canoes, sometimes to the annoyance of those who fish the loch from rowing boats or pottering outboard-motored dinghies. But there are still placid days when the loch lies quiet and deserted, days of dull drizzle when the fishermen are left in possession and occasions when a storm drives everyone off the water.

Dr. Johnson visited the loch in heavy rain and commented: "Had Loch Lomond been in a happier climate, it would have been the boast of wealth and vanity to own one of the little spots which it incloses." But tastes have changed and few now would wish to transform the ruggedness of the islands into "soft lawns and shady thickets."

*Loch Lomond viewed from the beach at Luss
with Ben Lomond dominating the horizon.*

*Cottages at Luss. A Highland Gathering is
held every summer in this little village on
the west shore of Loch Lomond.*

The lovely village of Luss on the western bank of Loch Lomond attracts many tourists who travel the main trunk road northwards. It is little more than a single street of small cottages leading to a landing stage and an attractive foreshore. Wordsworth and Coleridge stayed here in 1803, but they were not greatly impressed with the loch, which, to minds attuned to the Lake District, seemed too large an expanse of water. The church which serves the village was built by Sir James Colquhoun of Luss in 1875 as a memorial to his father who was drowned in the Loch. The Colquhouns (pronounced Kahoon) have deep roots in the district, for their seat south of the village at Rosdhu has been in the family since the fourteenth century, though their present residence is an elegant country house, built in the eighteenth century to replace the old castle.

Glen Luss and Glen Douglas penetrate westwards through steep hills to spectacular sea lochs, Loch Long with its branch, Loch Goil, and the Gare Loch. This latter is a busy yachting centre which also has a naval station, breaker's yards and an oil-tanker terminal.

Gare Loch is still emphatically Colquhoun country. At Garelochhead in 1853 there was a famous "battle" when Sir James Colquhoun and his gamekeepers were defeated in an attempt to stop trippers on a steamer excursion from landing on a Sunday. Helensburgh, at the foot of the Gare Loch where it joins the Firth of Clyde, was laid out by Sir James Colquhoun towards the end of the eighteenth century. It is now a Glasgow dormitory as well as a holiday resort and one of the chief yachting centres of the Clyde.

Loch Long and Loch Goil have the dramatic character of steep-sided fjords. Between them lies a peninsula of rough and rocky mountains ironically termed "Argyll's Bowling Green", which was part of the Ardgoil Estate given by Lord Rowallan to the City of Glasgow in 1906.

Loch Goil is a particularly attractive sea loch, which has been preserved from heavy tourist traffic by the fact that the road along its bank has no outlet, leading only to the sleepy village of Carrick with its ancient ruined castle, once a stronghold of the Argylls. No view in Scotland is more reminiscent of the smaller and quieter Norwegian fjords than that of Loch Goil from Carrick.

Lochgoilhead at the head of the loch is visited enough to give it a gentle stir without making it busy. It has an ancient and well-restored church and near at hand the wild road over to Loch Fyne through Hell's Glen. Eastwards the road to the head of Loch Long climbs to the summit of the pass above Glen Croe known as "the Rest and Be Thankful" from the rough stone seat at the summit thus inscribed. The modern road and the modern car take the sting out of the pass, but the old road still zig-zags below the modern one and is used for motor hill-climbing trials.

Ben Arthur, better known as "the Cobbler", which overlooks the pass, is famous for its rock-climbing, and its ease of access to Glasgow makes it increasingly busy as the sport grows in popularity. Arrochar, the tourist village at the head of Loch Long, is thronged with climbers all the year round for there is snow as well as rock-climbing in the mountains. Here Loch Long and Loch Lomond are separated by an isthmus only 1½ miles wide.

Loch Long, overshadowed by "the Cobbler" (2,891 ft.), so called because its profile looks like a cobbler sitting at his last.

Loch Restil, seen from "Rest and Be Thankful", with the new road beside it. The old road is still used for hill climbs.

*The tiny harbour
of Inversnaid
on the Eastern shore
of Loch Lomond.*

The road up the eastern shore of Loch Lomond is quieter than that on the west. From Drymen it winds to meet the Loch at Balmaha, a village with rows of yacht moorings just north of the mouth of the Endrick, then leaps the miniature Pass of Balmaha and continues along the shore to peter out at Rowardennan, the hamlet from which the towering Ben Lomond is usually climbed.

The other road access to the eastern bank of the loch is at Inversnaid, where the road follows a precipitous stream down to a tiny harbour and a hotel. It is a beautiful spot, where, in Gerard Manley Hopkins' words, "the darksome burn . . . flutes and low to the lake falls home" in a waterfall which drops directly into the edge of the loch.

The road from Inversnaid leads back to the modern tourist centre of Aberfoyle, running north of Ben Lomond and passing on its way close by Loch Katrine and along the peaceful Loch Ard, graced by small islands, one with the foundations of a castle, formerly owned by the 2nd Duke of Albany, who was beheaded in 1425.

Aberfoyle itself is famous for its association with Scott's *Rob Roy*, for it was to the Clachan of Aberfoyle that Frank Osbaldistone and Bailie Nicol Jarvie travelled to meet Rob Roy MacGregor. The modern hotel in the village is called the "Bailie Nicol Jarvie" and a plough coulter hanging from a tree opposite the hotel commemorates the bailie's fictional exploit.

The river alongside the road is the Forth.

The blossoming banks of Loch Ard seen from the Inversnaid to Aberfoyle road.

From Aberfoyle downwards the river meanders through a broad valley, well-farmed except where the deep and shifting Flanders Moss still preserves a winter refuge for migrating geese.

To the south of this strath lies a line of hills, the Campsie Fells, Gargunnock Hills and Kilsyth Hills which run from Killearn at the west to Stirling at the east and screen the agricultural Forth valley from the midland industrial belt. Killearn, a village expanded by houses built for prosperous country-loving Glaswegians, stands well on a foothill of the range strikingly marked by a monolith erected in honour of George Buchanan, the famous reformer and tutor to James VI, who was born in the village. Above Killearn rises the striking, detached Dumgoyne Hill in which the western part of the range terminates. Its characteristic shape, rather like the head of an elephant, makes it an unmistakable landmark when viewed from the highlands to the north, from Glasgow or from an aeroplane turning in to land at Abbotsinch airport.

These hills are astonishingly unspoilt, considering their proximity to Glasgow, and apart from the Campsie Glen, which always attracts picnickers and motorists, the roads are not busy. One can often park by the reservoir above the Loup of Fintry or on the smaller forestry roads which run through the hills to the north, and imagine oneself in a remote part of the Highlands; and the upper Endrick valley has much in common with the upland valleys of the quiet border country. Yet from almost every summit in the range the walker looking southwards can see on a clear day, if not the chimneys, the smoke plumes of Glasgow and Airdrie and Falkirk.

The Lake of Menteith at evening. In the background is the parish church of Port of Menteith, the only settlement on Scotland's only 'lake'.

Below, Loch Achray with the Trossachs Hotel on its shore and the slopes of Ben Venue (2,386 ft.).

Bottom, a steamer on Loch Katrine, which is 8 miles long but only an average of $\frac{3}{4}$ miles wide. Steamers go through the Trossachs as far as Stronachlachar at the western end of Loch Katrine.

Immediately north of the upper Forth and feeding it through a tributary lies the pretty Lake of Menteith, with wooded shores and three islands, on the largest of which are the ruins of the Priory of Inchmahome, founded in the thirteenth century by Walter Comyn, Earl of Menteith, for the Austin canons. In hard winters the lake freezes over, and is thronged with skaters and with those beguiled by the prospect of walking to an island. Invariably a large bonspiel is held on such occasions and there can be no finer setting for curling.

Northwards again across a range of rough but low hills is one of the great tourist areas of Scotland, centred on the Trossachs. The approach by road is from Aberfoyle over the twisting Duke's Road, from which one gets sudden and impressive views of Loch Drunkie and Loch Venachar. Loch Drunkie, more often viewed than visited, lies caught close in wooded hills with no access by road. The prospect of Loch Venachar is more distant, with the main road from Callander to the Trossachs running along its northern bank under the shoulder of Ben Ledi to join the Duke's Road beside Loch Achray, now a resort of water skiers.

The Trossachs—the word may mean "Thwart Hills"—is the gorge which lies between Ben Venue and Ben An and embraces the eastern end of Loch Katrine. It is splendidly romantic, a tumble of rocks and mounds clothed in fern and mixed woodland, leading to the end of Loch Katrine which lies enclosed by steep slopes and cliffs, a jutting crag cutting off from view the full length of the loch. It epitomizes the nineteenth-century taste in scenery.

Loch Katrine in the Trossachs, scene of Sir Walter Scott's poem 'The Lady of the Lake'.

The Trossachs and Loch Katrine are irrevocably associated with Sir Walter Scott, and particularly with *The Lady of the Lake*, formerly one of the most widely read poems in the language. In its opening the anonymous hunter, who is later revealed as the King of Scotland, pursues a stag, which takes refuge "in the deep Trossachs wildest nook," and leads him to a craggy vantage point,

Where, gleaming with the setting sun,
One burnish'd sheet of living gold,
Loch Katrine lay beneath him roll'd.

The Lady of the Lake comes across the water to him in a skiff, believing the sound of his hunting horn heralds the return of her father.

Today the slopes of the Trossachs, though still wild, are by no means untrodden, and Loch Katrine is the source of Glasgow's water.

From the pier at the Trossachs a lake steamer takes passengers up the loch to Stronachlachar on the road to Inversnaid.

The main trunk road north from Ardlui leads through Glen Falloch to Crianlarich, a small village serving as a tourist centre for the rugged and austere country of Glen Dochart and Strath Fillan. Legend firmly associates St. Fillan with this area. The saint was reputedly buried at St. Fillan's Priory, of which only the foundations remain, and in Fillan Water is St. Fillan's Pool, a holy pool with which a strange custom was associated. Lunatics were immersed in it and left overnight, bound on its banks. If they were found untied in the morning they were held to be cured, but if the knots were intact, a cure was believed to be hopeless.

The hills at Crianlarich, Ben More and Stobinian.

C

Below, Fort William, at the Southern end of the Caledonian canal, situated between the lower slopes of Ben Nevis and shore of Loch Linnhe. Bottom, Bridge of Orchy with Beinn Dorain (3,524 ft.) in the background.

Crianlarich is notable as the meeting point of two remarkable Highland railways, both of which have an interesting history.

The earlier of the two was the Callander and Oban Railway which was originally authorized in 1865, but constructed slowly and with difficulty. In those days the Highlands were remote and isolated and experience in building railways through such country was lacking. The difficulties were underestimated and by 1870, when seventeen miles of track had been laid alongside Loch Lubnaig to Lochearnhead and then up the difficult ascent of Glen Ogle, the company halted work owing to financial pressure. For some years the railway ran only to the barren Glenoglehead, surely the oddest terminus ever! It took three years to construct the straightforward line to Crianlarich and Tyndrum. There again progress halted, but Oban was too important a prize to be missed and by 1880 the line was finally completed. Recent closures have re-routed the earlier part of the Oban line, formerly via Callander, to follow the later course of the West Highland Railway. Begun in 1889 this linked Craigendoran and Fort William and was backed by the North British Company. The line runs high above Gare Loch and Loch Long, follows the west side of Loch Lomond from Arrochar northwards to Crianlarich and Tyndrum, takes a huge horseshoe sweep between Tyndrum and Bridge of Orchy and then crosses—often floating on ballast—the roadless wilderness of Rannoch Moor to Spean Bridge and thence to Fort William. Between 1897 and 1901 the line was carried on past Loch Eil and Glenfinnan to Arisaig, Morar and Mallaig. This line, it has been claimed, is the most beautiful rail journey in the world.

A lochan on Rannoch Moor. The West Highland Railway crosses the boggy parts of the moor on a brushwood base which is said to be floating.

Tyndrum, five miles north west of Crianlarich, sits at the junction of the roads to Oban and to Fort William in bleak countryside, marked with the remains of eighteenth and nineteenth-century lead-mining.

Near at hand is the place where tradition has it that Robert Bruce, who had retreated to Rannoch with the remnants of his army after his defeat at Methven, was ambushed by Macdougall of Lorne, as he tried to break southwards to link up with his supporters in the Bruce country of Dumfriesshire. Bruce escaped but in the struggle lost the elaborate and magnificent brooch known as the Brooch of Lorne.

The road from Tyndrum to Bridge of Orchy climbs to the watershed between the North Sea and the Atlantic and crosses the boundary from Perthshire to Argyll. Above Bridge of Orchy, a famous resort for fishermen, towers Beinn Dorain, 'peak of the streamlet'. The river descends the lonely and isolated Glen Orchy, westwards past waterfalls, to feed Loch Awe. Northwards, there are two roads, the old road built by General Caulfield in the aftermath of the '45, which is little more than a track beyond the inn at Inveroran, and the modern road, well-metalled, which skirts Loch Tulla, the small loch from which the river Orchy flows, and then strikes north into what must be some of the most awesomely desolate scenery in Britain.

To the west is the Black Mount, the Marquis of Breadalbane's deer forest, and between the road and Glen Etive there are at least seven summits of over 3,000 feet, sculptured by massive corries, among which, between Clach and Stob Ghabhar, is Coireach a' Ba, reputedly the largest in Scotland. In such country man is dwarfed.

35

Rannoch Moor, twenty desolate square miles of moor, bog and water.

To the east, beneath these towering peaks lies the bleak and desolate Moor of Rannoch, a reminder of a world unconquered by men. Diverge a little from the road—if the bog will let you—and the silent miles in front of you, unrolling to the shadowy outline of Schiehallion beyond Loch Rannoch, grip the imagination quite unforgettably.

R. L. Stevenson caught the spirit of Rannoch in *Kidnapped*: "as waste as the sea; only the moorfowl and the peewees crying upon it, and far over to the east, a herd of deer, moving like dots. Much of it was red with heather; much of the rest broken up with bogs and hags and peaty pools; some had been burnt black in a heath fire; and in another place there was quite a forest of dead firs standing like skeletons." It has changed little.

The barren Moor of Rannoch is for the northbound traveller the prelude to the more striking grandeur of Glencoe, the most famous of Scottish glens, both for its scenery and for its bloody memories. Here on 13th February, 1692, acting on orders of William III, Campbell of Glen Lyon and his soldiers massacred the Macdonalds of the glen after accepting their hospitality and living with them for twelve days.

The new road through the glen is less tortuous and sensational than the old, but it is still possible to gain easy access to the famous viewpoint, "The Study" (a corruption of the Scottish *stiddie* meaning 'anvil'), down by the old road. The falls are close by and most prominent are the Three Sisters of Glencoe, Beinn Fhada, Gearr Aonach and Aonach Dubh.

The paps of Glencoe towering above Glencoe village.

37

Below, the Ferry at Ballachulish. The deck is a hand-operated turntable which allows cars to drive straight off upon arrival.

Bottom, Port Appin, with a rough coastline northwards to Loch Linnhe. Castle Stalcair, scene of successive vendettas, lies off this coast.

Past the village of Glencoe, or more properly Bridge of Coe, which stands beneath the Pap of Glencoe, the western outlet from the glen leads to Loch Leven, a sea-loch not to be confused with the inland Loch Leven by Kinross. An island in the loch has an ancient burial ground with many Macdonald graves.

Where man is so dwarfed by nature it would be absurd to talk of an industrial area, but two small towns on the loch have in fact been founded on industry. Kinlochleven at the head has a large aluminium works, which was founded in 1908, and a modern hydro-electric scheme. Ballachulish at the neck of the loch is still scarred with memorials of slate quarrying, though the industry is now dead and the life of the place revolves round the busy car ferry which cuts off the long drive round the loch for motorists travelling between Oban and Fort William.

Loch Leven is an arm of Loch Linnhe, another sea loch, which marks the southern end of the Great Glen, properly speaking not a glen at all, but the great rift valley which divides Scotland in two.

The eastern bank of the Loch south of Ballachulish is the Appin country, the ancient seat of the Stewarts of Appin, who forfeited their lands after the '45. It was here that the famous "Appin Murder" of Colin Campbell of Glenure took place. A considerable mystery surrounds the identity of the murderer, though James Stewart, "James of the Glen" was hanged for the crime. The murder figures largely in Stevenson's *Kidnapped*, David Balfour being in conversation with Glenure when the shot is fired and consequently suspected as an accomplice.

Below, Port Askaig, Islay, looking across the narrow Sound of Islay to the Feolin Ferry on Jura.

Bottom, the Paps of Jura (over 2,500 ft. at the highest point). Jura is 30 miles long and a maximum of 9 miles wide, although the island is nearly divided by water at Tarbert.

Off the coast south of Loch Linnhe lies a group of islands of various sizes, the most southerly of the Inner Hebrides.

The largest of the group is Islay, famous for its malt whiskies, and once the administrative centre of the Lords of the Isles. The island is almost split in two by the deeply intrusive sea lochs, Loch Gruinart in the north and Loch Indaal in the south. The western part of the island, the Rinns, is famous for its coastal scenery, as is the Oa peninsula on the eastern part, with its savage cliffs. Two American troopships were lost off Islay with heavy casualties in 1918, the *Tuscania*, which was torpedoed, and the *Otranto*, which sank as a result of a collision. There are memorials to those who lost their lives, though many of the bodies have been removed.

Jura, Islay's near neighbour, is a comparatively unfrequented island with magnificent scenery, including the famous twin Paps of Jura, the highest points in this group of islands. Just north of Jura in the strait which separates the island from Scarba is the whirlpool of Corrievrechan, which figures in Scott's *Lord of the Isles*. It can be seen from Jura and its turmoil can be heard over a considerable distance.

Colonsay and Oronsay are smaller islands, joined at low tide, which stand to the north-west of Islay and Jura. Oronsay has the ruins of a fourteenth-century Augustinian priory on the site of an earlier Celtic foundation, and Colonsay has the beautiful sub-tropical gardens of Kiloran.

The vivid and thriving town of Oban on the mainland at the mouth of Loch Linnhe is the gateway to these Western Isles.

Oban

Oban is little more than 200 years old, but it has progressed considerably since Boswell and Johnson found "a tolerable little inn" there. Most of the expansion took place during the nineteenth century when Oban drew riches from the development of the tourist trade, and the town is now full of hotels, and in the summer is a lively and busy place.

The town enjoys a splendid position on pleasant, low hills overlooking a picturesque bay, which is sheltered by the island of Kerrera. The sunset over the mountains of Mull is famous, and the sheltered waters provide a centre for yachting, and a harbour for fishing vessels.

The houses of the town are ranged up the hillsides behind the hotels and shops of the Esplanade and harbour front. Each hill is crowned by a singular monument. On Oban Hill is the shell of an unfinished hydropathic, a late-nineteenth-century enterprise which foundered for lack of funds before the building was complete. On Battery Hill is "MacCaig's Folly." At the close of the nineteenth century a local banker, John Stewart MacCaig, started to build at his own expense a museum with a look-out tower, intending the project to provide work for the unemployed. But work was abandoned when MacCaig died and this building, like the hydropathic, was never completed. They were ruins from birth.

Oban has plenty to offer the visitor. It is a convenient centre for mainland touring, as well as for the famous sailings to the Western Isles, and it is an interesting town in itself, lively with boats and fish auctions. It is also host to the Argyllshire Highland Gathering in late-August, a meeting which draws thousands of visitors.

Clachan bridge, grandiosely termed 'The Bridge Across the Atlantic'. The road goes through to the southern end of Seil Island.

South and inland of Oban lies the district known as Lorn. A favourite coastal excursion is to Seil Island which lies close to the coast a short distance south of Oban. It is separated from the mainland by the narrow Clachan Sound, which is crossed by a hump-backed bridge. Since the Sound is in fact part of the Firth of Lorn which is an arm of the Atlantic Ocean, the bridge is often described as the bridge across the Atlantic.

Inland lies Loch Awe, which is reached by the Pass of Brander under the steep slopes of Ben Cruachan. Here in 1308 the MacDougalls attempted to ambush Robert Bruce, but came off worse in the exchange, one of the battles celebrated in Barbour's poem, *The Bruce*.

Loch Awe itself is one of Scotland's best-known lochs. Nowadays, it is famed for the beauty of its scenery and the excellence of its salmon and trout-fishing, but its past was more stormy. Originally a centre for several clans including MacArthurs, MacGregors and MacNaughtons, the last of whom owned the now-ruined castle at Innisfroach, it became in the end a Campbell lake, a barrier protecting the Campbell heartland.

The Loch has several islands, the largest the isle of Inishail, with the ruins of a convent. Two have ruins of castles. The one on Innischonain was once a royal stronghold under the keeping of the MacArthurs. The other, on Kilchurn, now linked to the bank by marshes, was founded by Sir Colin Campbell of Glenorchy in the fifteenth century and was extended in the sixteenth and seventeenth centuries. It is a romantic ruin in a striking setting close to the towering bulk of Ben Cruachan.

Kilchurn (pronounced Kilhoorn) Castle. This magnificent ruin inspired a poem by Wordsworth. One of the towers was felled by the hurricane which destroyed the Tay Bridge in 1879.

Crinan Bay, with Craignish Point in the distance. This is the western end of the canal which was begun in 1793, but not completed until 1817 under the direction of Telford. In the early years of its use there was a passenger service from Ardrishaig by horse-drawn boats.

From Oban there is suspended southwards the long peninsula of Kintyre, dividing the Firth of Clyde from the Atlantic and presenting such a barrier to navigation that it has been pierced by the Crinan Canal, running $8\frac{1}{2}$ miles from Loch Crinan on the Sound of Jura to Ardishaig on Loch Gilp, a small arm of Loch Fyne.

This must be one of the pleasantest canals in the world. Since its purpose is to cut off the long sea voyage, it is not an industrial canal, but winds through meadowland broken by low hills and rocks, its banks scattered with brambles. At both ends it has splendid views over open water.

Nowadays the traffic is confined to smaller fishing boats, elegant Clyde yachts and puffers, and the small coastal vessels which serve the minor piers and harbours. At the Crinan end is an attractive basin, cradled in hills, where there are always ocean-going yachts berthed. At the southern end is the little Loch Fyne port of Ardrishaig.

Loch Fyne is the longest of the fjorded sea lochs, joining the Firth of Clyde, just north of the Isle of Arran, with the Kilbrannan Sound. This gives access to the North Channel and the Sound of Bute leading south-eastwards to the Firth of Clyde. The Loch itself used to be famous for its herring fisheries, based on Ardrishaig, but the industry has declined to the point where one suspects some of the fishmongers' notices of "Loch Fyne Kippers." It seems that more Loch Fyne fish are sold than are taken from the water.

Centre, a 'puffer' on the Crinan Canal.

Bottom, Inveraray, the historic capital of Argyll, seen across Loch Fyne.

Inveraray Castle, seat of the Dukes of Argyll, and early model for the Scottish Baronial architectural style.

Inveraray, which stands on Loch Fyne at the mouth of the Aray, is one of the most attractive small towns in Scotland, and is the Campbell seat. The greater part of the old town was burnt by Montrose in 1644, and the town was rebuilt under the patronage of the Dukes of Argyll in the eighteenth century, the planning and building being shared by William Adam and his son John, Roger Morris and Robert Mylne. The result combines dignity with great charm.

It is significant that Dr. Johnson found here "an inn, not only commodious, but magnificent."

Inveraray Castle, the seat of the Dukes of Argyll, stands just outside the town. It is an extraordinary example of the neo-Gothic. The interior mixes Augustan and Romantic.

Southward from Crinan are the districts of Knapdale and Kintyre, almost separated from each other by the deeply intruding sea loch West Loch Tarbert, which all but meets the small indent of East Loch Tarbert. So narrow is the isthmus that Magnus Barefoot, who was granted lordship over the islands by treaty, had himself dragged across the strip of land in a boat in order to claim that he had circumnavigated the "island of Kintyre."

The peninsula ends in the Mull of Kintyre, where a steep and rocky descent leads to an eighteenth-century lighthouse.

A little north of this extremity, with an excellent sheltered anchorage on its indented bay, lies the largest town of Kintyre, Campbeltown, founded under James VI's policy of colonizing the Highlands.

The Mull of Kintyre whose lighthouse is only thirteen miles from the coast of Ireland.

Loch Screscort, Rum. The island is noted for its golden eagles and herds of red deer. It is possible to land here, but permission to stay the night must be obtained from the Nature Conservancy Board.

North again, up the Atlantic coast is a scattered collection of islands of the Inner Hebrides, reached by steamer from Oban or Mallaig.

Farthest out of these is Tiree, "the kingdom whose heights are lower than the waves", the flattest of all the Hebrides and in the past the granary of Iona. Nowadays the sunshine and good weather have been turned to account by a bulb-growing industry. Tiree is notable for the extraordinary, excavated prehistoric broch, Dun Mor Vaul, on its northern coast. This ancient fortress dwelling is thirty-five feet in diameter with chambered walls thirteen feet thick.

Tiree's neighbour, Coll, also has a notable monument, the almost intact fortress castle of the MacLeans at Breachacha towards the south end of the island. Coll has a rocky and forbidding east coast, but is nevertheless a fertile island.

North of Coll and Tiree lies a small group of islands, best known perhaps from the sound of their names—Canna, Rum, Eigg and Muck. Canna is most important to the Highlander because it is the only island owned by a Gaelic-speaking laird of Scottish birth, who is attempting to preserve the culture and way of life of the island in the face of great difficulties of communication. The steamer routes tend to miss the island.

Rum is the direct contrast. Rugged and impressive, it is short of arable land and after depopulation in the early nineteenth century, it became an absentee sportsman's private park. Since 1957 it has been a nature conservancy. Eigg and Muck to the south are both beautiful and romantic islands, where the old life struggles on, in the case of Muck, with rare steamer connections to the mainland.

Staffa, literally 'The Island of Staves or Columns', with cliffs rising 135 feet above the sea. Fingal's Cave can be visited by steamer from Iona or Oban.

By contrast with these islands there lie to the south two smaller islands whose good communications are almost entirely due to the interest they hold for tourists, namely, Staffa and Iona. In Staffa nature has made the monuments: in Iona they have been made by man.

Staffa, which is uninhabited, has magnificent cliffs and caves of columnar basalt, including the famous "Fingal's Cave", celebrated by Mendelssohn in his *Hebrides Overture*.

Iona has a very different history. Here, in 563, St. Columba landed from Ireland and from the island undertook the conversion of Scotland. It is the cradle of Scottish Christianity, and has consequently evoked much sentimental response from writers and painters. Dr. Johnson's measured comment is still the best because it is the most robust: "We were now treading that illustrious Island, which was once the luminary of the Caledonian regions, whence savage clans and roving barbarians derived the benefits of knowledge, and the blessings of religion. To abstract the mind from all local emotion would be impossible, if it were endeavoured, and would be foolish, if it were possible. . . . That man is little to be envied, whose patriotism would not gain force upon the plain of Marathon, or whose piety would not grow warmer among the ruins of Iona!"

The religious life of Iona has recently been revived. Just before the Second World War the Rev. George MacLeod founded the Iona Community, which has undertaken restoration of the ruined Benedictine abbey, which, in the sixteenth century, served as cathedral for the See of Argyll. Now church services are held on this island rich in ruins and relics stretching back to the dawn of Christianity.

Iona Cathedral, the Chancel. Iona was the burial place of many Scottish monarchs, including Macbeth.

Tobermory, the main town of Mull, has a quayside of charm and dignity.

Mull is the largest of the Inner Hebrides, and contains great diversity of scenery—a mountainous centre, rough moorland to the north, lochs, the sandy machair at the top of the Ross of Mull, and a coastline so indented that it measures about 300 miles. Dr. Johnson wrote at some length of the hardships of life in Mull, where the Clearances and emigration led to a tremendous depopulation, but there are some signs of a partial revival and symbolically, Duart Castle, confiscated in the Killing Times after Culloden, is now again the home of the chief of the MacLeans, having been repurchased and restored.

David Balfour, shipwrecked on Erraid, waded across to the Ross of Mull at low tide, and crossed the island, where he had his famous meeting with the blind catechist.

Tobermory, the main town of Mull, has an attractive situation on a bay and is a pleasant little place. It was developed by the British Fisheries Society in the late eighteenth century but fishing is now much less important than the tourist industry.

Tobermory Bay is famous for its sunken wreck, that of a Spanish galleon from the Armada, reputedly laden with treasure and blown up and sunk by a Scottish hostage held on board. Salvage attempts have been made since the seventeenth century and the lure is still strong today, modern operations being conducted in the full glare of newspaper publicity.

Coll and Tiree, Rum, Eigg and Muck, Mull itself and even, on a clear day, the Outer Hebrides, may be viewed from Ardnamurchan.

Ardnamurchan Point, the westernmost point on the mainland of Scotland.

D

49

Ardnamurchan, Sunart, Ardgour and Morvern form what is virtually a promontory, bounded on the south-east by Loch Linnhe, on the south-west by the Sound of Mull and on the north by the Atlantic and by Loch Shiel.

David Balfour crossed from Mull to Morvern by a ferry from Torosay to Kinlochaline, encountering on the way an emigrant ship at which voyagers to America were being given a last tearful farewell from friends and relatives on the beach. Car ferries now take the same route, passing at the entrance to Lochaline the ruins of Ardtornish Castle, built about 1340 and for a century and a half the headquarters of the Lord of the Isles. The castle, dominating the rocks that flank the sea and backed by steep cliffs with picturesque waterfalls, is a ruin in the best romantic tradition.

Strontian, a village close to the head of Loch Sunart, has, by contrast, a modern relevance which has sinister undertones, since it gave its name to the element strontium, now associated with contamination from atomic explosions, and first discovered in the lead mines of this area in 1790.

Ardgour is a mountainous district, stretching from Loch Linnhe to Loch Shiel, and famous mainly as a sporting centre. The hamlet of Ardgour is at the Corran Ferry which crosses Loch Linnhe about ten miles south of Fort William, the strategically placed West Highland centre standing under Scotland's highest mountain, Ben Nevis (4,406 ft.), on the south-eastern shore of Loch Linnhe. The town, which is an important communications centre and tourist resort, is mainly Victorian and a product of the railways, but its origin goes back to a fort built by General Monk in 1655.

Northwards across Loch Shiel from Ardgour lies Moidart. We are in the heartland of the '45.

Prince Charles Edward set out with two ships from Nantes on 22 June, 1745, to regain the throne of Scotland for the Stuarts. One of his ships was so damaged by the English that it had to limp back to France with its precious cargo of arms. In the other Charles Edward landed first on Eriskay, and later on the Moidart peninsula, "without men, without money, with but seven friends of my own," as he said. These companions are known as the Seven Men of Moidart.

At first the Prince met with little support, but after he had won to his cause Macdonald of Clanranald and Young Lochiel of the Camerons, others followed. On 16th August the Jacobites had their first success when the Macdonalds captured eighty men of the Royal Scots who were marching to Fort William, and on the 19th the Marquis of Tullibardine raised the Prince's standard at Glenfinnan, at the head of Loch Shiel, as a rallying point for the clans. Thus began the disastrous but romantic adventure which led to the tragedy of Culloden.

A monument erected in 1815 by MacDonald of Glenaladale, grandson of one of Prince Charles's supporters, marks the place where the clans rallied and serves as a memorial to those who died for the cause. Close by in the loch lies St. Finnan's Isle, with its ruined chapel, appropriately enough an ancient burial ground of the Clan MacDonald.

Glenfinnan is a beautiful and romantic place where, as in the case of Iona, memories are inescapable. In this spot they are of intense loyalties and bitter disasters.

Loch Eil, with Ben Nevis towering in the distance.

The road to the isles passes Glen Finnan after following the northern bank of Loch Eil, an arm of Loch Linnhe. From the head of the loch one looks back at a splendid view, dominated by Ben Nevis.

To the west is the route to Arisaig. Northwards along the coast stretch the famous silver-white sands, usually known as the Sands of Morar. The village of Morar stands on a narrow strip of land separating from the sea the inland Loch Morar. At 180 fathoms this is by far the deepest inland water in Britain and with the exception of one lake in Scandinavia the deepest in Western Europe. On one of the islands in the loch, Simon, Lord Lovat was captured. Hogarth sketched him as he passed through St. Albans on his way to London to be tried and executed.

The mainland end of the traditional road to the isles is Mallaig, which stands at the mouth of Loch Nevis. This is the terminus of the West Highland Railway, which reached the village in 1901, and of the modern motor road. The life of the place centres on the railway station and the harbour. It is a port of call for the steamers which ply to both the Inner and Outer Hebrides and there is a ferry across to Armadale in the Isle of Skye. Mallaig is very much a sea-going place with important herring fisheries and trawlers and seine-netters catching a wide assortment of white fish such as plaice, lemon sole, dab, eel, conger and dogfish. The railway makes it possible to get the produce of the sea and of the Mallaig lobster ponds to market, but there is also a modern deep freeze plant.

Mallaig harbour crowded with the small craft of local fishermen and holiday makers.

53

The Western Islands of Scotland have the incalculable advantage that they are usually reached with the romance of a sea journey. In the case of the nearer islands like Bute, Mull and Skye, three-quarters of an hour is sufficient to cross the Kyle; but the journey from Mallaig to Lochboisdale, on the South Uist, takes three times as long and the voyage on one of the MacBraynes' Royal Mail Ships across the Minch to Stornoway is a five-hour affair.

Fortunately, there is an extensive steamer and car-ferry service available to the tourist and motorist. Since 1964 the three sister ships R.M.S. Clansman, Columba and Hebrides (each one 229 ft. long and 2,104 tons gross) have been operating a modern drive on/drive off ferry service to Mull (from Oban), to South Uist (from Mallaig) and to Harris (from Mallaig via Skye), which makes the mysterious beauty of these islands more accessible than ever before.

MacBraynes also run a fleet of twelve Royal Mail ships which take passengers to all the well-known islands and many of the lesser-known ones like Canna (to the South of Skye) and Gigha (off the Kintyre peninsula).

Round tours by train, steamer or coach (or a combination of all three) can also be taken, to while away an afternoon or a fortnight.

The other Scottish centre of pleasure steamers is the Firth of Clyde, and here their history goes back to the very beginnings of steam navigation.

Although Henry Bell was not strictly the inventor of the steamship, there is no doubt that the *Comet's* maiden voyage in 1812, when capitalism was still in its lusty infancy, set a trend which has made the Clyde world-renowned for shipbuilding.

Thirty-eight years after James Watt, who held an appointment at Glasgow University, had made the first steam engine, Bell fitted out a 42-foot wooden hull with a small $4\frac{1}{2}$ h.p. engine, paddlewheels, and a tall funnel which also supported a sail, Viking-style. Amazingly, for Bell was no engineer (the *Comet's* engine was a larger version of one used to pump sea water into the swimming baths at his Helensburgh hotel), the venture succeeded, and daily voyages were made to Greenock and later through the Crinan Canal to Fort William, Oban and Appin. Within months a rival steamer of more efficient proportions was also plying the waters of the Firth.

As shipbuilders began to use iron for hulls of increasing size, men from the Highlands and from Ireland flocked into the Glasgow area to work in the shipyards. At the same time they swelled the body of travellers on steamships as they escaped out to the Firth at weekends or Public Holidays. The rivalry between the steamship companies became so intense that three or four steamers would be racing each other to the jetty at Gourock or Dunoon for a single berth.

Now the number and variety of steamers are less, but leisurely journeys can still be taken past the famous yards at Clydebank out to Rothesay, the Kyles of Bute or to Ardrishaig, at the mouth of Loch Fyne.

Undoubtedly the most famous of the islands on Scotland's western coast is Skye, a bait for tourists drawn by the exciting lure of its torn shape on the map and by the many romantic accounts of its mountains and mists, sea lochs and castles. It is an island rich in legends and famed for its hospitality.

Celtic Skye was taken over by the Norsemen, and its place names tell of its Scandinavian connections, though after the defeat of the Norwegians by Alexander III at the Battle of Largs, it was restored to Scottish rule under the Macleods of Dunvegan. The chiefs of Skye formally kept out of the Jacobite rising of 1745, but as the Skye Boat Song recalls, the island figured largely in the events of that time.

> *Speed bonnie boat like a bird on the wing,*
> *"Onward" the sailors cry;*
> *Carry the lad that's born to be king*
> *Over the sea to Skye.*

At the time when Prince Charles Edward Stuart was a fugitive in hiding it was to Skye that Flora Macdonald brought him from Benbecula, disguised as her woman servant, Betty Burke. Flora is buried on the island.

Skye today is still predominantly Gaelic-speaking in everyday life and is deeply religious and Sabbatarian in temper so that tourists who create disturbance on a Sunday— or even who move from one lodging to another—may lose the warmth and friendliness of welcome which is in the nature of Skye folk.

Kyleakin is Skye's doorstep, and its castle, Castle Moil, is said to have been built by the daughter of a Norwegian king, who married a Macdonald, and who stretched a chain across the Kyle in order to levy a toll on ships.

The main road from Kyleakin runs along
the northern coast to the village of Broadford,
where a secondary road of great scenic
beauty branches away to the south-west. It
runs through the small hamlet of Tomin at
the foot of the Red Hills, round the head of
Loch Slapin, and across the peninsula to
Elgol, famous for its views of the Cuillins,
the islands of Rum, Canna and Eigg and the
mountains of the mainland. From its tiny
harbour, which lies far below the village, a
boat can be hired to cross Loch Scavaig to
Loch Coruisk, the "cauldron of water."

Loch Coruisk is a dramatic and desolate
stretch of water, more easily reached by sea
than on foot. It is trapped under the looming
Cuillins, a place where nature awes the
onlooker as it did Alexander Smith:

"The utter silence weighs like a burden
upon you; you feel an intruder in the place.
The hills seem to possess some secret; to
brood over some unutterable idea which you
can never know. You cannot feel comfortable
at Loch Coruisk, and the discomfort arises in
a great degree from the feeling that you are
outside everything—that the thunder-splitten
peaks have a life with which you cannot
intermeddle."

The Cuillins themselves are the most
precipitous and dramatic of British mountains
offering a challenge to the rock-climber and
exhilarating ridge scrambling to the
experienced mountain walker. There are
fifteen peaks over 3,000 feet and since they
rise almost from sea level and are subject to
whirling mists, their height gives little
indication of their power. Even visitors from
countries where 3,000 foot peaks are considered
hills would never deny the Cuillins the name
of mountains.

Right, Dunvegan Castle on the shore of Loch Dunvegan, overlooking a bay full of islands.

Bottom, the Cuillin range seen from Loch Sligachan. The name Cuillin is an old Norse word meaning 'keel-shaped'.

The north-west of Skye beyond the Cuillins is less mountainous, but the coast is rugged and indented by two large sea lochs, Loch Bracadale and Loch Dunvegan. On the latter of these Dunvegan Castle, one of the most romantic of monuments, occupies a rocky prominence.

Dunvegan is the seat of the Macleod chiefs and is world famous. It reputedly dates from the ninth century and the buildings, still inhabited, date from the fifteenth to the nineteenth century. Originally, it could be entered only from the sea, making it an impregnable stronghold, but now that visitors are likely to be friendly there is access by a bridge across the ravine that was formerly a protective moat.

Amongst the relics preserved in the castle are the two-handed sword and two-bottle drinking horn of the famed Rory Mor, Sir Roderick Macleod, the 12th chief. It is said that he could drain the drinking horn at one draught. The "fairy flag", another prized possession of the castle, is said to have been captured from the Saracens during a Crusade.

But Dunvegan has long been famous, not merely for its historical relics, but for the elegance and wholeheartedness of its hospitality. From early times, the MacCrimmons, the hereditary pipers to the Macleods, established a primacy among pipers which testified to the joys of the hall. Dr. Johnson responded warmly, as Boswell tells us: "Our entertainment here was in so elegant a style, and reminded my fellow-traveller so much of England, that he became quite joyous. He laughed, and said, 'Boswell, we came in at the wrong end of this island.' " The tradition is still maintained in the modern, urbane and civilized interior.

Portree lies on the east coast of Skye on a small sea loch. The name means King's port and dates from a visit of James V.

Portree, capital of Skye, is a pleasant town of whitewashed houses, many of them boarding houses or hotels.

Northwards lies the peninsula of Trotternish, the most northerly of the island, ringed by a road, which for the most part follows the coast. Just north of the town, however, it runs alongside Loch Fada and Loch Leathan and by the broken and

pinnacled ridge which forms the backbone of Trotternish. Here is the Old Man of Storr, a sensational 160 ft. pinnacle, not climbed until 1955.

Further north near Flodigarry is a monument to Flora Macdonald and on the western coast of the peninsula at Kingsburgh there used to stand a house where she and the prince sheltered.

Barra and the adjacent islands of Vatersay, Mingulay and Berneray lie at the southermost extremity of the chain of the Outer Hebrides. Barra is a peaceful island of soft colours with beautiful Hebridean sands and a rocky coast. It is a true crofting community, predominantly Catholic and wholly Gaelic-speaking, and the people are famous for their charm and their stories.

To the north, South Uist is similar in character, again predominantly Gaelic, Catholic and crofting. It has a strong military tradition and has fostered many great pipers. The decision of the British government in 1955 to set up a rocket range at Eochar appeared to threaten the island, but in fact, it has made little impact and the island remains unspoiled.

A thatched cottage on South Uist with a pile of peat blocks drying in the sun.

61

Benbecula, joined by road to the North and South Uists.

Benbecula, the small island which lies between South Uist and North Uist, is nowadays a communications centre for the Southern Outer Hebrides. It has an airport, originally built for the R.A.F., with direct links to the mainland, and a viaduct to South Uist, built during the last war, together with a causeway to North Uist completed in 1961. It is now possible to drive from the airport to Kilbride at the southern tip of South Uist or to Suenish at the northern point of North Uist.

The island itself is almost as flat as Tiree, but is so patched with a multitude of small lochs where brown trout thrive that, from the air, it could almost be taken for an archipelago. The population of Benbecula bridges the Free Kirk Protestant northern islands and the Catholic South Uist and Barra. Held together by the Gaelic tongue the people of both religions live side by side in exemplary amiability.

North Uist, though geographically linked through Benbecula to the Southern Isles and separated from Harris by the Sound of Harris, is in culture rather part of the Northern Outer Hebrides. It is a Protestant island with the usual Scandinavian element in its population. Like Benbecula, it is scattered with lochs and lochans and offers superb sport with salmon as well as brown trout and sea trout. It also attracts the archaeologist and anthropologist for it is rich in standing stones, stone circles and chambered cairns from the remote past, as well as minimally-adapted black houses from a more recent, but disappearing, culture. To the north of Sollas on the sandy Udal, a unique late-medieval settlement has been excavated.

North Ford, North Uist. The causeway across the shallow channel to Benbecula was built in 1960.

A cottage spinning-wheel being used in Plocrapool, Harris.

In spite of a considerable land boundary with Lewis, stretching from Loch Resort to Loch Seaforth, Harris by a geographical and historical oddity rates, and rightly rates, as a separate island. The people are probably more Celtic than the Norse Lewismen, and the land is rougher, in parts fretted and torn like the scenery of another planet.

Lewis is remarkable as a Gaelic-speaking community of about 30,000 with a peasant economy which has successfully met the modern age and is incomparably thriving and prosperous, showing its vigour both in its industry and in its culture. It shares with Harris the domestic Harris tweed industry and important fisheries. Lord Leverhulme's notorious entrepreneurial excursion into Lewis and Harris life, which ended disastrously in the short term, probably acted as a worth-while stimulus in making the island what it is today, confident as it looks outward at the world, yet independent and tenacious of its own character. Perhaps the strong Norse roots of the population have something to do with it. Certainly Lewis bears strong resemblances to the vigorous coastal communities of northern Norway.

Stornoway, the capital town of Lewis, lies in a sheltered bay on the eastern coast of the island. It is the only Gaelic town of its size and was built in the Georgian era by the Lewismen themselves rather than by outsiders. Now the town is a shopping and educationl centre with the well-known Nicholson Institute, which equips the islanders to go up to university. It has an important hospital, is the home of the most prominent Hebridean newspaper and is well-provided with churches and hotels. In short, it is the nearest we have to a truly Gaelic metropolis.

The harbour at Stornoway.

The Five Sisters of Kintail, one of Scotland's most dramatic ranges.

The steamer from Stornoway returns us to the mainland at Kyle of Lochalsh, the point to which the Skye ferry from Kyleakin also plies. This is the terminus of the railway from Inverness and contrasts with Stornoway in the way that its roots stretch back inland and eastward.

The natural line of travel lies along the main road which leads to Inverness through Kintail Forest to Loch Cluanie, beyond which it forks, south to Invergarry or north to Invermoriston and up along the western shore of Loch Ness.

It is an attractive road, particularly in its northern stretch as far as Cluanie Inn. The Five Sisters of Kintail rise dramatically above the road in the heart of the Mackenzie and Macrae lands.

Just to the south of Kyle of Lochalsh, the road follows Loch Alsh and then, in superb scenery, the shore of Loch Duich. Close to the junction of Loch Duich and Loch Long, on an island linked to the mainland by a causeway, lies the picturesque and romantic Eilean Donan castle.

Eilean Donan dates from the middle ages and is indeed thought to occupy the site of a Caledonian vitrified fort of very early date. Its past has been troubled. For the greater part of its history it was the stronghold of the Mackenzies of Kintail, but it was reduced to a ruin in 1719 when English ships subjected it to heavy bombardment in order to subdue a Jacobite garrison of Spanish troops under the command of the 5th Earl of Seaforth. The castle was restored between 1912 and 1932.

Eilean Donan, a medieval castle which today serves as a war memorial for the clan MacRae.

It is the road to Strome Ferry we shall take, the main route until the new road is completed, which crosses Loch Carron and lands at a pier overlooked by the fragmentary ruin of Strome Castle. From there the way leads along the northern shore of the loch to the village of Lochcarron or Jeantown, where the road to Shieldaig and Applecross strikes off. The Applecross road climbs steeply over the Pass of Kishorn to the sea loch of the same name and then detaches itself from the Shieldaig road to climb through hairpin bends up the Pass of Bealach-nam-Bo. The road is narrow and steep, reaching over 2,000 ft. above sea level and offering superb views to all but the driver, who is too occupied to look.

It is the character of this road that has earned Applecross the reputation of being the most inaccessible place on the mainland of Scotland, and beyond the little village itself are scattered houses which can be reached only by footpath. In the seventh century Mael Rubha, an Irish monk from the community at Bangor, founded a monastery here and there are still remains of an ancient church as well as a graveyard with a Celtic cross. Certainly, Mael Rubha chose well, for this is not merely a remote and peaceful place, but also a beautiful one looking out on Raasay and Skye across the water of the Inner Sound.

From Applecross Bay the road turns south along the coast through the tiny hamlet of Camusteel to peter out at Toscaig at the head of Loch Toscaig. The steamer service which once called from Kyle of Lochalsh is now withdrawn and Toscaig is even more remote than Applecross itself.

Below, Shieldaig. The name is Gaelic for 'herring bay' and describes the traditional occupation of this village.

Bottom, the north end of Loch Torridon with the skyline punctuated by weathered dome-shaped peaks of red sandstone.

The road to Shieldaig, like that to Applecross, used to end at the village, but it has now been driven through as part of the plan for a scenic coastal route up the west. Shieldaig itself is a pleasant waterside village on a sealoch, from which a path leads to the crofts along the northern coast of the Applecross peninsula.

Beyond the village the road now runs through to Torridon over Bridge of Balgy, skirting delightful, quiet little bays on the southern shore of Upper Loch Torridon, which is separated from the main loch by a narrow strait. At Ploc of Torridon, a promontory in the loch, are three rows of flat stones facing a larger standing stone. This strangely intimate and living monument is known as the Church of Ploc and services have been held there.

Near the hamlet of Torridon at the head of the upper loch is Torridon House and behind it to the North a famous deer forest. A branch road with no outlet runs along the north shore through Inveralligin to Diabaig on the main loch. From there only a rough track persists along the quiet coast until it meets the road south at Redpoint.

The coast northwards beyond Opinan is an extraordinary tangle of sands and strange dunes with flat tops covered in close grass, as flat as billiard tables. Crofts are strung out, many of them deserted. On a summer's day this is a glorious place to bask or bathe: but when the mists blow in across the Minch the whole landscape has an incomparable mystery and desolation. It has one of the remotest of all the Scottish youth hostels, the isolation no doubt a great part of its attraction.

Beinn Eighe, part of a nature reserve of 10,000 acres from Loch Maree to Loch Clair.

In the hinterland, and towering over Loch Torridon itself, lie the great mountains of the Torridon range, of which the main peaks are Liathach, Beinn Eighe, Beinn Alligin and Beinn Dearg. All but the last top 3,000 feet and the range offers splendid climbing and sensational ridges. The reddish purple sandstones of the area have contributed the type name, Torridonian, which is used by geologists to describe this pre-Cambrian group. Botanists can find a very wide range of vegetation, including rare alpine types, and as well as the usual range of animal and bird life, there are natural red deer, eagles, pine martens and the true Scottish wild cat. Beinn Eighe is the centre of the first National Nature Reserve in Great Britain, declared in 1951.

Immediately to the north, one of the main roads east reaches the coast at Gairloch. This is an area famed for its sands, especially Big Sands on the north of the bay, but there are so many superb beaches that nowhere in Britain is one more likely to find sands and solitude together.

Loch Ewe, another larger bay immediately to the north, was used by the Navy in both world wars and the entrance to the loch is still partly blocked by anti-submarine nets. There is a naval defence depot at Aultbea.

In addition to the naval station and the tourist trade, there have been experiments, centred on the village of Inverasdale, to mount schemes for the revival of crofting, partly by setting up a small supplementary industry.

View across Gairloch bay with Baoisbheinn and Beinn Alligin in the distance.

It may sound as if the Loch Ewe area is spoiled by naval works and industrial experiments, but this is far from being the case. The scarring is slight, and is amply compensated by the fact that on a promontory in the loch is one of the most delightful spots on the west coast, the almost magical garden of Inverewe.

The garden, which is now in the care of the National Trust for Scotland, was founded by Henry Osgood Mackenzie in 1864 and further developed by his daughter. It is now one of the outstanding tourist attractions of the West Highlands.

When Osgood Mackenzie started work on it the site of the garden was a barren, rocky headland, virtually bereft of vegetation though enjoying a climate rendered mild and virtually frost-free by the Gulf Stream. Sheltering belts of trees were planted to keep out the gales which blew in from the Atlantic and soil was imported in creels. Mackenzie experimented with a variety of plants, and succeeded in laying out a most delightful garden in which a good deal of the vegetation is exotic and sub-tropical. One of the most impressive aspects of the garden is its continuity of development, by now over more than a hundred years. Windbreaks had to grow before it could be properly planted and many of the trees and plants took time to mature.

Now, as well as the splendid display of rhododendra, there is a wide variety of plants ranging from Australian tree ferns to climbing hydrangeas and agapanthus. And Mackenzie boasted of his apples, pears and plums. One of the magnolias, 28 feet high and 75 feet in circumference, is thought to be unrivalled for size anywhere.

Gruinard Bay, 4 miles across, has a shoreline studded with coves of pink sand. The bay is also noted for its flounders which attract large seabirds. No camping is permitted in the area.

Osgood Mackenzie wrote a pleasant autobiography, *A Hundred Years in the Highlands*, which the fame of his garden has helped to keep in print. Most of it is concerned with his life as a sportsman and with Highland lore, but he gives an account too of his work at Inverewe of which he is charmingly proud, as the following shows:

"Now I turn to the flowers, and I think almost anything that will grow in Britain will grow with me. I was once in a garden in a warm corner of the Isle of Wight in June, when my hostess and I came upon a gardener carrying big plants of agapanthus in tubs from under glass to be placed out of doors. His remark as we passed him was, "I think, my lady, we may venture them out now," and I could not refrain from answering the old man back: 'If not, then I do not think much of your climate, for in the far North of Scotland we never house them, nor even protect them in winter. I have had great clumps of agapanthus in the open for thirty years and more, and the white, as well as the blue variety, flowers magnificently every year'."

There are few sources of pride less objectionable than pride in a garden which gives joy to many. After Osgood Mackenzie's death his daughter Mrs. Mairi Sawyer carried on his work in the garden, then in 1952 it was bought by the National Trust for Scotland.

The coast road leaves Loch Ewe at Aultbea, and strikes across the neck of land that separates the loch from Gruinard Bay, where a beach of fine sand runs along the road. On the western arm of the bay is a delightful but isolated crofting community with one of the most melodic names in Scotland, Mellon Udrigle.

71

Plockton

Although the boundary which separates the administrative county of Ross and Cromarty from that of Sutherland lies still a little to the north beyond the two Loch Brooms, yet it is fair to say that the coast of Wester Ross from Plockton in the South to Mellon Udrigle and Gruinard in the north already has a special character of its own.

North of Loch Broom the coast is wilder, rockier and more broken, more given to cliffs and steep slopes. The mountains are less solidly packed against the coast, more isolated and not so high.

What is typical of Wester Ross is a certain type of crofting village which, whatever one may think of it in winter, has in summer even in rainy weather a softness and secure snugness that is less common as one moves northward.

As a background to these villages there are hills, or more often high mountains. But the land along the water's edge is green and relatively fertile, and the villagers have been encouraged to build close to the shore. Types of such villages are Plockton, on Loch Carron, and Shieldaig, on the arm of Torridon.

Their well-built and well-slated little houses are trim and whitewashed, and on still summer days are mirrored in the water. Many of them have been sadly depopulated, but with the coming of better roads there is a flicker of new life in them. True, much of any new prosperity will come from tourism rather than fishing and crofts, but we must console ourselves with the thought that at least some of the tourists will be the grandchildren of emigrants whose nostalgia dwelt upon just such harbours and villages.

73

Below, Slioch (3,217 ft.) with Loch Maree at its foot. Giant salmon and sea trout have been taken from the loch.

Bottom, Destitution Road, winding its way across the moors near Dundonnell, with An Teallach (3,484 ft.) in the distance.

The most prominent feature of inland Wester Ross is Loch Maree, a splendid stretch of water 12½ miles long and 2¼ miles at its broadest point. Much of its bank is wooded and in its broader reaches it is dotted with islands. One of these, Isle Maree, contains ruins which are said to be those of a chapel serving as a hermitage for St. Mael Rubha, the Bangor monk who founded the early religious community at Applecross. The waters of the well on this island were reputed to cure madness.

If we add to wooded shores and islands excellent sea-trout fishing and a setting in rugged and beautiful mountains, then it is easy to think of Loch Maree as a northern equivalent of Loch Lomond, less accessible and consequently less crowded. Maree's dominant mountain, in spite of the adjacent bulk of Beinn Eighe, is Slioch, which rises abruptly and dramatically from the waters of the loch to a height of over 3,000 ft., furrowed with gullies and visible at once from base to summit.

Loch Maree at its northern end is separated from the sea only by a narrow neck of land at Poolewe, and it was probably at one time a sea loch. It forms one of a pattern of four parallel valleys, the southernmost Loch Torridon and the two north of Loch Maree, Little Loch Broom and Loch Broom.

The southern shore of Little Loch Broom is traversed by the road from Gruinard, which has to turn back on itself and drive south-east. Across the loch looms Beinn Ghobhlach and close to the road both at the lochside and higher in Strathbeg are beautiful waterfalls one of which is the well-known Ardessie Falls.

Corrieshalloch Gorge and the Falls of Measach.

Above Little Loch Broom lies the hamlet of
Dundonnell and nearby it a hunting lodge
serving Dundonnell Deer Forest. The road
here is known as "Destitution Road", a
name which reflects the intense sufferings of
the Highlands in the potato famines of
1846-7 and 1851. The construction of the
road was undertaken as part of a programme
of relief through public works, the destitute
Highland labourers being paid in food only.
In the dire circumstances that led to the
making of this road many people of the area
emigrated to the United States, Australia or
New Zealand. To those who stayed and
suffered the road is a fine monument, rising
to 1,110 feet and commanding outstanding
views of one of the most picturesque
mountain ranges in Scotland, the strangely
shaped sandstone peaks of An Teallach, "the
Forge."

Close by the woods of Braemore House,
this road from Little Loch Broom joins the
main trunk road running north-westwards
from Inverness and Dingwall to Ullapool.
Near the junction and just to the west of the
main road is the sensational Corrieshalloch
Gorge, a corrie unusual in being eroded in
schist rather than in sandstone. The canyon
is sheer-sided, about 200 feet deep at its
maximum, and running to over a mile in
length. A suspension footbridge has been
thrown across the gap for the benefit of
tourists and from it they can peer down into
the giddy depths of the narrow gorge and see
the Falls of Measach crashing into its head.
The sensational nature of the experience is
heightened by the presence of a notice on the
bridge warning the public that no more than
six people should stand on it.

Loch Broom, a sea loch 21 miles long, opening into the Minch.

Below the gorge, the road follows the River Broom down to the head of the loch, where Lochbroom Kirk stands on the farther bank of the river. Then it takes the eastern shore of the loch running beneath the bulk of Meall Dubh and Beinn Eilideach with a splendid view of Ben More Coigach ahead as it approaches Ullapool.

The loch had long been a fishing ground when Ullapool village was founded in 1788 by the British Fisheries Society as a station for both herring and white fish. After a decline in the nineteenth and early twentieth centuries, there came a revival in the Second World War when the attraction of Ullapool was increased by the ruining of East Coast waters. The village is now a busy centre for the fishing fleet in the winter.

The site of Ullapool, on a gracious sweep of shingly bay, the trailing edge of a spit of land thrust out into the loch, was well chosen, and the fact that it was a planned development gives it a pleasing unity. The original plans, and indeed the design of some of the individual houses, were reviewed by the famous Thomas Telford. It remains restrained and charming.

As a tourist centre, Ullapool has much to commend it. The good access by a relatively fast main road to Inverness makes it the most accessible point on the north-west coast, tempting those with time for only a short visit. There is good walking and pony-trekking in the surrounding hills, as well as excellent angling and good sea-fishing, which is gaining popularity.

The whitewashed houses of Ullapool, diversified occasionally by red sandstone, scattered out along Loch Broom side.

77

Lochinver, at the head of its loch. The town is a notable resort for tourists and anglers, since there are more than 200 fish-bearing lochs in the neighbourhood of the town.

Lying off from Ullapool at the mouth of Loch Broom are the Summer Isles, which are virtually uninhabited, though they provide some rough grazing. In former times Tanera More, Priest Island and Norse Island were inhabited. Now the seals and the birds are in command.

Yet the islands have a special claim on the affections of many who have never visited them through the books of the naturalist F. Fraser Darling, who restored the facilities and lived and farmed for some years on Tanera More. Darling's description of the islands he knew more intimately than anyone else cannot be bettered:

"No other group of Scottish islands is quite like the Summer Isles; they are very rough and broken, covered with peat rather than soil, except where the red rock itself bursts through the black of winter and the green of summer in numerous cliffs, scarps and slabs. They are on an open seaboard, yet among them may be found quiet, unruffled anchorages. How delightful it is after crossing the rough water in a westerly wind from Glas Leac Beag to the north end of Tanera Beag to turn south into the narrow sound between that island and Eilean Fada. The water is flat, yet two or three hundred yards away across the island the roaring sea of the Minch can be heard falling on the bay of big shingle and rattling the boulders up and down. Here in the narrow sound are little red cliffs where rowan trees cling and festoons of fragrant honeysuckle lie over the heather."

This is the eternal dream of islands made true for the many by a man with the skill and courage to wrest a living from one.

North of Ullapool is a substantial peninsula between Loch Broom and Eddrachillis Bay comprising the districts of Coigach and Assynt. Particularly in the northern district the land is thickly splattered with small lochs interspersed with steeply rising, isolated mountains. The coast itself has an island remoteness in many parts.

In the south, Achiltibuie, the crofting township and small resort which is strung along the mainland coast of Badentarbat Bay opposite the Summer Isles, is only to be reached by the most circuitous road, and when the westward track peters out at Reiff there still lie away to the north the cliffs and lochans of the uninhabited Rubha Mor.

Lochinver is the largest and most accessible place in the district of Assynt, though it is no more than a small fishing village which does not rate a population figure in guidebooks.

There is a bus a day to Lairg and the cargo boat from Glasgow puts in every ten days. This may present problems to local people, but most of the visitors who are attracted to such an area are looking for peace and beauty. They find it here in a village built along the tranquil sea loch waterside in well-wooded surroundings. And they have also the convenience of a hotel.

From Lochinver the secondary road snakes northwards with frequent sharp turns and steep hills, hugging the coast as closely as rough country will allow, and then cutting across the neck of the crofting peninsula of Stoer to follow the north coast through Drumbeg to Kylesku. At Clachtoll, near Stoer, there are cairns and a broch which testify to the antiquity of human settlement in what nowadays seems an isolated area until the summer visitors fill the sandy coves.

(l. to r.) Cul Mor (2,786 ft.), Suilven (2,399 ft.), and Canisp (2,779 ft.), outcrops of ancient gneiss rock, seen across Loch Inver. Suilven is a Gaelic name meaning 'column mountain'.

The rocky shores of Loch Assynt, scene of the betrayal of the Marquess of Montrose.

Just north of Lochinver a road strikes inland to Inchnadamph, climbing the rushing River Inver to Loch Assynt. Ahead is the serrated ridge of Quinaig and to the south the isolated peaks of Canisp and Suilven, 'the sugar-loaf mountain', a famous landmark for sailors.

Loch Assynt itself, seven miles long, owes the charm of its scenery to the variety of rocks along its shores and to the ruin of Ardvreck Castle. It was the seat of Macleod of Assynt and the place in which James Graham, Marquess of Montrose, was taken after his defeat at the Battle of Carbisdale. There is still dispute as to whether Macleod of Assynt captured Montrose on the moss and handed him over to the authorities or handed him over after entertaining him in apparent friendship, tempted by the reward of £25,000.

North from Assynt we jump temporarily ahead, following the road as it curves alongside the river Laxford and up to Loch Stack, passing under Ben Stack and Ben Strome and looking across Loch More to the great Reay Deer Forest whose highest point is Ben Hee.

From Laxford Bridge there runs to the South-east the most northerly of the main roads which strike diagonally across Scotland to join east coast and west coast. The river Laxford, whose name derives from *laks*, the Norse word for salmon, is, not surprisingly, a fisherman's river. The road follows the river closely through bare and desolate country to Loch Stack one of whose islands once provided a summer residence for the chief of the clan MacKay.

The glittering white quarzite screes on the slopes around Loch Stack are a distinctive landmark.

F

Kylesku, the point where Lochs Cairnbawn, Glencoul and Glendhu come together, with Beinn Leoid dominating the horizon.

From the shore of Loch Assynt the main road strikes northwards, climbing a pass with Glas Bheinn to the east and the strikingly pointed Quinag to the west and offering superb views before it descends to Kylesku Hotel and ferry. Just east of Kylesku, Loch a' Chairn Bhain, across which the ferry boat plies, divides into Loch Glendhu and Loch Glencoul. Towards the head of the latter, accessible only on foot or by boat, is the waterfall Eas Coul Aulin, which, at 658 feet, contends for the title of the highest in Britain.

The north end of the ferry is at Kyle Strome, and from there the road heads north-westwards to the coast, offering views across the strewn islands of Eddrachillis Bay and Badcall Bay towards the Point of Stoer.

Scourie is an irregularly-spread crofting village with a hotel which caters for the anglers who enjoy brown trout fishing in the innumerable small lochans which dot the area. The local mansion, Scourie House, has a sheltered garden which testifies, with its palm trees, to the mild influence of the Gulf Stream on this northerly west coast. The house was once a Mackay seat and the seventeenth-century general, Hugh Mackay, was born there.

Below, the road from Kylesku with distant Quinaig (2,653 ft.) catching the evening light.

Below, the road from Kylesku with distant Quinaig (2,653 ft.) catching the evening light.

Bottom, Lairg at the southern end of Loch Shin. The loch, 17 miles long, has been greatly deepened by a dam near Lairg and is well-known for its trout and salmon.

The island of Handa, off the quiet coast about two miles north-west of Scourie, rises in cliffs of red Torridonian sandstone up to 400 feet. It is uninhabited, the nesting place of guillemots, puffins and razorbills, and is now a nature reserve managed by the Royal Society for the Protection of Birds. The Society maintains a bothy on the island for the use of its members who go to study the bird life. Another attraction of Handa is its caves.

The road follows the northern bank of Loch Shin, the largest loch in Sutherland, seventeen miles long, whose level has been raised by a dam at its south-eastern end, part of a vast hydro-electric scheme in which the loch serves as a reservoir.

Lairg, at the lower end of Loch Shin, is a holiday resort and tourist centre, which is particularly important because of its position on a junction of roads which run northwards to Tongue and Bettyhill, westwards to Lochinver and Laxford Bridge, eastwards to Brora and Golspie and southwards to Inverness. The village has become a terminus for a variety of bus routes to remote Highland places. A little to the north of the village a monument on a hillside commemorates the "Great Plough", used by steam cultivators when almost 2,000 acres of land were reclaimed between 1873 and 1877 by the Duke of Sutherland.

On the road south, which follows the River Shin to Invershin, are the spectacular Falls of Shin, where crowds gather to watch the salmon leaping when they are running up river. Across the river from Invershin the pretentious baronial Carbisdale Castle, completed in 1914, dominates the river and the Kyle.

Sandwood Bay, one of the beautiful beaches at the lonely northern tip of Scotland.

The north-western extremity of Scotland offers the most isolated coastal scenery on the British mainland. The approach from the south by a branch road from Rhiconich, just north of Laxford Bridge, peters out at Balchreick to leave a five-mile walk through totally uninhabited country to the superb beach of Sandwood Bay. Further north there is an uninhabited coast of cliffs stretching to Cape Wrath. A ferry across the Kyle of Durness gives access to a roadhead, but the ferry does not carry motor vehicles and, once across, the traveller depends upon a very irregular motor which runs from the ferry to the lighthouse across the bleak moor of the Parph, once famous for its wolves, and still quite untouched by the hand of men except for the one rough road.

The lighthouse at Cape Wrath was built in 1828 at a cost of £14,000. It stands on cliffs and the light, 400 feet above sea level at high tide, is visible for twenty-seven miles.

Eastwards from it the northern coast of Scotland presents an exciting diversity, its pattern of steep and broken cliffs and sea-washed beaches being broken by the sea lochs, Kyle of Dunness, Loch Eriboll and Kyle of Tongue. The visitor who, in a good summer, is fortunate enough to strike a heatwave period, wins solitude and privacy of an exceptional kind.

And even in bad weather the cliffs are impressive. Kennageall or Whiten Head, for example, between Loch Eriboll and Kyle of Tongue, rises 1,935 feet from the sea and is fretted with caverns worn by the waves.

Kennegeall cliff rears up nearly 2,000 feet over the solitary coast between Loch Eriboll and Kyle of Tongue.

85

Thurso, seen across the river of the same name. Many fine Georgian houses are still standing as a tribute to the far-sighted civic schemes of Sir John Sinclair.

The towns and villages of the north coast are also attractive. Of these the largest is Thurso, enjoying a pleasing situation on Thurso Bay, whose wide sweep of sands is sheltered by the tall cliffs of Holburn Head and Clardon Head. To the north-east the splendid Dunnet Head, the most northerly point on the Scottish mainland, is visible in the distance across the opening of Dunnet Bay.

Thurso is a town distinguished for its architecture and continues to care for its tradition by thoughtful restoration. In the old streets near the harbour, the fishermen's cottages, which date for the most part from the 17th and early 18th centuries have been carefully and charmingly restored. In the Georgian era, the Thurso-born Sir John Sinclair laid out a new town of broad streets round the square which bears his name, so that Thurso has a planned distinction like that of Edinburgh's New Town, though on a more intimate scale.

In older times Thurso was important for its sea link with Scandinavia and indeed its name is said to mean "Thor's River". The link is even symbolized botanically for in these islands the northern holy grass, common in Norway, grows only on the banks of Thurso River.

The chief industries in the past were fishing and quarrying Caithness flags, the great flat flagstones of rock which are a feature of local field divisions, although formerly used for the pavements of cities. This industry has greatly declined despite modern attempts to revive it, and recent development in the area is largely due to the foundation of the nuclear reactor establishment at Dounreay, which is pioneering the production of electricity by nuclear power.

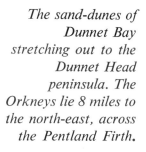

The sand-dunes of Dunnet Bay stretching out to the Dunnet Head peninsula. The Orkneys lie 8 miles to the north-east, across the Pentland Firth.

Below, the broken coastline near Durness.

Bottom, a view out through the mouth of the Cave of Smoo. Trout are said to live in the pool within, which is fed by a waterfall entering through a vertical roof-shaft.

Caithness, though it can claim to be the most northerly county of Scotland, is not a Highland county. It has virtually no Gaelic and has more in common with the north-east coastal area around Aberdeen than with the Celtic west. The Scandinavian influence, however, is much stronger.

Travelling westwards along the coast beyond Dounreay, one moves into Sutherland again and into the Highland world. Bettyhill, for example, is a product of a Highland clearance. It was "founded" by Elizabeth, Countess of Sutherland, to accommodate tenant crofters she wished to evict from Strathnaver in the interests of sport. The village has neither good soil nor good anchorage for a fishing fleet, and thrives today only on the tourist trade and anglers.

Durness, the village lying most westerly on the coast, is really a group of small crofting communities. Balnakeil House nearby was formerly a summer residence of Lord Reay, and before that of the Bishops of Caithness. The churchyard has a grave with a remarkable epitaph:

> *Donald Mackmurchor hier lyis lo:*
> *vas il to his freind var to his fo:*
> *true to his maister in veird and vo.*

A couple of miles to the east of Durness is the Cave of Smoo, which was much admired by Sir Walter Scott. The cave, which is in limestone cliffs, opens out of the rear of a deep cove. The outermost of three chambers is entered through an arch 53 feet high and is 203 feet long and 120 feet broad. A second cave is inaccessible except to those prepared for a caving expedition and has a waterfall descending into it with a drop of 80 feet. Beyond, there is a third chamber.

Kyle of Tongue.

It is only between Durness and Tongue that the hinterland offers scenery of classic highland grandeur. At the heads of the valleys of Strath Dionard and Strath More, the Reay Deer Forest spans a range of hills from Foinaven in the north to Ben Hee in the south. The river Naver runs down Strath Naver to Bettyhill from a loch fed partly from Ben Hee and partly from Ben Klibreck and Ben Armine. These mountains, rising to summits approaching or just surpassing 3,000 feet, are seldom climbed and much of the ground is given over to sport.

Nearer the coast are Ben Hope and Ben Loyal which give to the Kyle of Tongue and the little village on it a true West Highland flavour.

Although geologically the Highland Line runs from Stonehaven on the east coast to the northern shore of the Firth of Clyde, there is within the mountainous area a real division of spirit.

The Western Highlands, comprising that part of Inverness-shire north and west of the Great Glen, Wester Ross and Western Sutherland, are the true home of the mainland Gaelic culture and in this they are linked to the Hebridean Islands. It is a culture infiltrated from the east but still surprisingly vigorous. It expresses itself in language and song, in angling and shinty, but perhaps most of all in the character of the people and their sense of community.

Argyll to the south and parts of Perthshire have remnants of the same culture but both have been much more assimilated to the English-speaking south and east. The Campbell influence gives Argyll a special flavour, and one which does not commend itself to every clansman's palate.

Excavations at Skara Brae. The site, which may be 3,000 years old, has revealed dwellings connected by covered passageways, as well as furniture, ornaments and even skeletons.

There is yet another northern world quite distinct from the Highlands. Across the Pentland Firth lies Orkney, and almost fifty miles farther north, Shetland.

The key to an understanding of the Northern Islands and their people is their very close link with Scandinavia. In ancient times they were part of the Norwegian dominions founded by the Norsemen, and in the late fourteenth century they became subject, as did Norway, to the Danish crown. It was not until the end of the seventh decade of the fifteenth century that they passed to Scotland as pledges given by King Christian I of Denmark for the payment of his daughter's dowry. The pledges were never redeemed, but many Orcadians and Shetlanders regard their islands as still only in pawn to Scotland.

Orkney is a county of islands, twenty-one of which are inhabited. By far the largest of these is Mainland, which contains the capital city of Kirkwall as well as the other main town and port of Stromness. Kirkwall itself is a confident, thriving northern town with a very Scandinavian flavour about it, as the name of its twelfth century Cathedral of St. Magnus might well suggest.

Just to the south of Mainland, caught in a ring of islands of which the main ones are Hoy, Burray and South Ronaldsay, is the sheltered water of the great naval base of Scapa Flow, which was used in both world wars. Here in 1919 the German fleet scuttled itself on surrender.

The main islands are linked by four causeways called Churchill's Barrier, originally constructed to keep out German submarines.

The most remarkable thing about Orkney to the unfamiliar outsider is that, though Orcadians are naturally accomplished sailors at home on water, Orkney is predominantly an agricultural community pursuing efficient farming by modern techniques.

The Earl's Palace, Kirkwall, built by Earl Patrick Stewart in 1607. The cruelty of the Earl (nearby Scalloway castle is said to be built with mortar made of eggs and blood) made the islanders wish for a return to Norse rule.

Orkney is extremely rich in historical monuments particularly from the prehistoric era. The most important are the huge chambered cairn of Maeshowe dating from *c.* 1500 B.C., the Standing Stones of Stenness and Ring of Brogar, and the incomparable Skara Brae, a beautifully preserved neolithic settlement about 3,500 years old, complete with stone furniture.

Shetland, though not so prolific of monuments as Orkney, has the famous broch of Mousa, forty-five feet high, and in the complex ruins of Jarlshof, continuously occupied from the bronze age until the seventeenth century, probably the most interesting single site in Britain.

Shetland is more scattered and far-flung than Orkney and consists of nearly a hundred islands, about twenty of which are inhabited. On the Mainland are the capital, Lerwick, and nearby the older capital of Scalloway. Lerwick is solidly rather than stylishly built, with the Scandinavian atmosphere of the Northern Islands. The contact with Scandinavia is also reflected in the festival of 'Up Helly Aa' at which about 300 men follow a replica of a Norse Galley and the Guizer Jarl dressed as a Viking chief. The occasion, on the last Tuesday in January, is to welcome the return of the sun.

Among other Shetland islands of interest are Fetlar, where Shetland ponies are bred, the barren Yell, second in size to the Mainland, Unst, the most northerly of the group with nothing between it and the Pole, Foula, isolated to the west some 16 miles into the Atlantic, and often cut off by high seas, and Fair Isle, famous for knitting and hand-loom weaving.

Although the Shetlanders breed sheep, cattle and ponies, and practise a little agriculture, they are fishermen with crofts rather than crofters.

91

The Up Helly-Aa, or Norse Festival of Fire celebrating the last hours of the malignant trolls and the return of the sun. Since 1885 a galley has been built for the sole purpose of making a spectacular blaze.

Dornoch Bay, with the hills of Easter Ross rising across the sands.

Wick, the county town of Caithness, has regular routes to Lerwick both by sea and air, and shares a Scandinavian influence with the islands, though in a milder form. It is still a busy fishing port, though the industry has declined since 1914. One of the newer industries is Caithness glass.

Southward on the east coast of Sutherland is a group of villages, originally the resort of crofters cleared from the interior, but now holiday places.

Across the Fleet from Golspie just north of the deep indent of the Dornoch Firth lies the tiny county town of Sutherland, Dornoch, with a cathedral partly restored during the nineteenth century, a renowned golf course dating from the early 17th century, and splendid sands.

The county town of Ross and Cromarty, Dingwall, lies at the head of the Cromarty Firth. "Ding" is derived from *thing,* the Norse word for parliament, a sufficient hint of an important early settlement on the spot, and the town's status as a royal burgh reputedly goes back to 1226. The town house in the main street dates from 1730, but the new county buildings are as recent as 1965. As an administrative centre, Dingwall keeps up-to-date.

Dingwall's neighbour, Strathpeffer, provides something of a contrast, having been a fashionable spa until the First World War. After a decline, the pump room was reopened in 1960 and the village is still a favourite holiday centre. Just north of the village is Castle Leod, seat of the Earl of Cromartie.

Castle Leod. Highland games are held on the first Saturday in August in its lovely gardens.

Sir Thomas Urquhart (1611-60), classicist, linguist, mathematician, translator and Lord Baron of Cromarty. A fervent Royalist, he was knighted in 1641, the same date as this frontispiece was engraved for a collection of his epigrams.

Immediately to the south of Dingwall and Strathpeffer lies the Black Isle, which is not an island at all but a peninsula moated by the Firth of Cromarty and the Moray and Beauly Firths. It derives its name from the tradition that it is seldom snow-covered. The old name of the peninsula was Ardmeanach, and interestingly enough Mary Queen of Scots granted Darnley the lordship of it.

Cromarty on the outer point of the peninsula was county town of the extraordinary county of that name, comprising the scattered lands of the Earls of Cromartie, until Ross and Cromarty were combined in 1891. Fortrose, the other main town of the peninsula, is a port in decline but a growing holiday centre.

Cromarty boasts two interesting sons. Hugh Miller was born in a thatched cottage in 1802. He worked as a stone-mason until he was thirty-three, devoting himself to writing, reading and natural history. He became established as a geologist through his book, *The Old Red Sandstone,* and won fame as an editor and pamphleteer; but he wore himself out in the controversy surrounding the Disruption of the Kirk, and in 1856 shot himself.

Sir Thomas Urquhart of Cromarty was a seventeenth-century eccentric of quite a different stamp. Educated at King's College, Aberdeen, well travelled and familiar at court, he spent much of his life suffering as a Royalist or dodging creditors. He produced epigrams, "a most exquisite table for restoring triangles", a pedigree tracing the Urquharts back to Adam, a plan for a universal language and the classic translation of Rabelais. He died abroad in 1660, it is said from a fit of laughter which seized him on hearing of the Restoration of Charles II.

Right, The Black Isle, a small peninsula between the Firths of Beauly and Cromarty. Boasting some of the richest farmland in the North, it gains its name from the fact that its earth is seldom covered with snow.

Bottom, St. Andrew's Cathedral (1866-9), seen across the River Ness.

Beauly, at the head of the Beauly Firth and hence of the Black Isle, is a pleasant place as its name, deriving from *beau lieu,* might well imply; but there is a rough history behind it. Just outside the town is Beaufort Castle, the seat of the Frasers of Lovat. It dates from the nineteenth century, the previous Fraser seat, Dounie Castle, having been razed after Culloden. It was, of course, associated with the famous and wily Simon, Lord Lovat, who for his part in the '45 was executed in London, the last British peer to suffer execution for high treason.

The major town in the area is Beauly's neighbour Inverness, which is often known as "the capital of the Highlands". Not only is it the administrative centre for Scotland's largest county, but it also contains government offices with regional interests. At the same time, partly because it has imported many of its present inhabitants, Inverness is not really a Highland town. In this it is comparable with many capitals. It is no more typical of the Highlands than London is of England.

Inverness has always been a communications centre. The road system of the Highlands runs west or north-west through the valleys and the town stands at the meeting of the ways. Eastwards there is ready access to the north-east lowlands and the Great Glen carries the main road to Fort William. The harbour, now used mainly for cargo, formerly had a considerable passenger traffic, and a link to the west is made by the Caledonian Canal. The railway age brought connections through both Aberdeen and Perth, and the airport at Dalcross has services to Glasgow, Stornoway, Orkney and Shetland.

The simplicity of the new bridge contrasts with the Victorian suspension bridge, once the main thoroughfare across the river.

The town is, of course, a historic one, but most of its older buildings have disappeared, or have been radically altered, like Queen Mary's House in Bridge Street, which is the oldest dwelling in the town. The name commemorates, not ownership, but a visit in 1562. The castle is a nineteenth-century building, though the older castle, possibly once that of Macbeth, may well have occupied the same site. The graceful new bridge, built in 1961, succeeds several others, the first a wooden one destroyed by the Lord of the Isles.

Not surprisingly Inverness is also an educational centre with its Royal Academy, an historic secondary school, and a Technical College as well as the North of Scotland College of Agriculture.

Inverness is an excellent touring centre with striking Highland scenery on its doorstep. Through Beauly there is access to the deep glens, Glen Farrar and Glen Affric whose watersheds lie almost at the west coast. Glen Affric, was once a main route to the west.

A still more famous tourist attraction lies on the very doorstep of the town, namely, Loch Ness. Its world-wide fame—or notoriety —comes from its monster. There are legends about such a monster going back to the seventh century but there have been many recent claims of sightings, some supported by rather ambiguous photographs. Systematic explorations have been made but so far with no positive results. A monster disposed to be elusive should have plenty of scope in a loch 24 miles long and 700 feet deep!

Glen Affric, its wild beauty unaltered by its hydro-electric scheme and afforestation.

Close by Inverness on the southern bank of the Moray Firth lies one of Scotland's smallest counties, Nairn. The county town, which bears the same name, is now a seaside resort sometimes called "the Brighton of the North", though in fact a quiet and relatively unfashionable place. Dr. Johnson wrote of Nairn: "At Nairn we may fix the verge of the Highlands; for here I first saw peat fires, and first heard the Erse (Gaelic) language".
It is true that at that time half of Nairn was Gaelic-speaking and half English-speaking so that the town was a meeting place of Highland and Lowland.

The encounter of the two in another guise casts a sombre shadow in this area. On the eastern outskirts of the town is the site on which Cumberland camped before marching west to Culloden Moor.

The battle fought there on 16th April, 1746, was the last to be fought on British soil, and a desperate and bloody affair it was. In forty minutes 5,000 Highlanders under Prince Charles Edward Stuart were defeated and routed by Cumberland's army of 9,000. Cumberland gave orders for the slaughter of the Highland wounded, and fleeing Highlanders were ridden down and killed like beasts. Even innocent citizens of Inverness suffered as the army ran amok. The Butcher Cumberland will never be forgotten in the Highlands, and never mentioned without horror.

Between Nairn and Culloden Moor is another place traditionally associated with a deed of horror. The Castle of Cawdor, in which Shakespeare set the murder of Duncan by Macbeth, dates from the mid-fifteenth century, though there are sixteenth and seventeenth century additions and the interior was remodelled in the nineteenth century.

Well of the Dead, Culloden Moor—one of the stones laid for each of the clans who fought for Bonnie Prince Charlie.

98

The harbour at Lossiemouth, built halfway through the last century to accommodate the growing fishing fleet.

To the east of Nairn stretch the extraordinary Culbin Sands, which, before the efforts at reclamation mounted by the Forestry Commission, were a shifting sand-dune six miles long and two miles wide, often known as the Sahara of Scotland. Fertile land was probably overwhelmed by blown sand late in the seventeenth century, perhaps as a result of the use of the stabilizing marram grass for thatching.

This is a coast of fine sands. Lossiemouth, just a little further along the coast, is famous for its great beaches. It is a thriving little town with an important Royal Naval Air Station, a tourist trade, and a busy fishing fleet, which enjoys a reputation for modern attitudes and innovation. Ramsay MacDonald, the first Labour Prime Minister, was born and educated in the town.

Buckie, too, has fine beaches, but the town itself lacks the character and identity of Lossiemouth, most of its development having taken place in modern times. It is significant that its charter as a burgh was only granted in 1888.

By contrast, the county town, Banff, is one of the most ancient in Scotland. It lies at the mouth of the Deveron which is spanned by a fine seven-arched bridge. Until the twelfth century, Banff belonged to the Northern House of trading seaports. Its castle, of which only traces now remain, was built to provide a defence against Viking raids and was a royal residence in the twelfth century.

The town is terraced above the harbour and in the older parts there are fine, dignified seventeenth and eighteenth-century burghers' houses. In the eighteenth century the town became a fashionable watering-place, and the world of fashion brought graceful buildings.

Elgin Cathedral, formerly one of the most splendid in Scotland and still a lovely and impressive ruin.

Old Elgin comprises three parallel streets running east and west, which were linked with cross-wynds. The High Street, still retaining many houses from the seventeenth and eighteenth centuries, runs from the royal castle on Lady Hill, at the west end, to the cathedral sanctuary at the east. The most interesting of Elgin's buildings is Thunderton House, just off the High Street, once a splendid town mansion. Prince Charles Edward lodged here shortly before Culloden.

The pride of Elgin, however, is the splendid cathedral, now in ruins, which was once the most graceful in Scotland. Most of the work is thirteenth century or earlier and the choir and east end, with its great rose window, are masterpieces of early Gothic.

Buchan, the exposed north-eastern district of Aberdeenshire, is dominated by twin fishing ports, Fraserburgh and Peterhead.

The larger is Peterhead, a stern granite town, once the centre of Scottish whaling and now devoted to herring and white fishing.

Peterhead and Fraserburgh were both founded in the sixteenth century, Peterhead by George Keith and Fraserburgh by Alexander Fraser. The castle Fraser built is now capped by the light of Kinnaird Head lighthouse, constructed in 1787, the first work of the Commissioners of Northern Lights. Fraserburgh was also for a short time a university town, the charter being granted in 1595, but the foundation collapsed when its first principal was arrested for taking part in the General Assembly of 1605.

Fraserburgh harbour crowded with fishing vessels displaying their fascinating tackle.

A wide sweep of the river Spey near Craigellachie. At either end of Strath Spey there are large, imposing rocks called Craigellachie ('rock of the strong place'). The one at the other, south-western end of the valley is near Aviemore.

The inland area of Moray and Banff is dominated by Strathspey, the broad lower valley of the Spey, which flows on or near the boundary between the two counties and enters the sea at Spey Bay between Lossiemouth and Buckie. Strathspey, a familiar name for the most graceful and elegant of Scottish dances, is called after it.

Towards the foot of Strathspey, before the river flows out on to the coastal plain, is a pattern of valleys formed by the Spey, the Fiddich and the Isla, an area famous for whisky.

Craigellachie, which lies at the junction of the Fiddich and the Spey, is a village terraced above the rivers. As well as its distillery and cooperages it has a large hotel and is a tourist centre. One of the features of the village is Thomas Telford's graceful single-span iron

bridge, flung across a pool in the river. Craigellachie stands at the edge of the lands of the Clan Grant, whose war cry, "Stand fast, Craigellachie", is echoed in a modern whisky brand name.

The capital of malt-distilling is, however, Dufftown, which lies a few miles to the east at the confluence of the Dullan and the Fiddich. An old jingle compares Rome and Dufftown, the first built on seven hills, the latter on seven stills. The town was founded and laid out by James Duff, 4th Earl of Fife, in 1817. The nearby Mortlach Church is a relic of a much earlier age. The church dates from the twelfth century but it is said that the foundation goes back to the sixth century when St. Moluag came from Lismore and according to local legend set up a church, a school and a farm.

Below, The mash tun—where the water and malted barley are mixed.

Bottom, The exciseman and the distiller check the specific quality of a blended whisky sample.

The Gaelic-speaking Celts called whisky *uisge-beatha*, "the water of life," and revered it as a remedy and consolation in frailty, adversity and depression. Now Scotch whisky is famous the world over.

The ancient way of making whisky is to soak and malt barley and dry the malt over a peat fire. The dried malt is bruised or ground and then mixed with hot water. When the mixture has cooled, yeast is added and a weak alcohol called "wash" is produced by fermentation. The wash is then twice distilled in copper pot-stills of traditional shape, first in the "wash-still" and then in the "spirit-still". The spirit which emerges, after it has been matured—for a legal minimum of three years, but often for much longer—is Scotch Malt Whisky. Such whiskies are often called "straight Malts," and they carry the characteristic flavour, body and fragrance which lie at the heart of Scotch whisky.

Malt whiskies tend to be expensive, and the most commonly-drunk whiskies are "proprietary blends" of malt whisky and patent-still whisky. Patent-still whisky can be made on a larger scale than malt whisky. Since it is made from maize or other grain with only a little malt barley, it is usually called Scotch Grain Whisky. It has a high alcoholic content, but is thin in body and has little flavour, though its aroma is mild and fragrant.

The blends of malt and grain used in the proprietary brands are kept consistent by using whiskies from the same distilleries and by the skill of the blenders, who pass their secrets on from generation to generation, so that you can buy your favourite brand all over the world.

Loch Morlich

At the head of Strathspey lies Grantown-on-Spey, a pleasant Georgian town laid out by Sir James Grant in the second half of the eighteenth century. Grantown is a centre for the tourist trade, which has changed its emphasis and is booming. Whereas in the nineteenth century, it was a health resort where people went to enjoy the air of the hills, and later—as it still is—a fishing resort which lures anglers with a bait of Spey salmon, it is now a ski-ing centre into which a quarter of a million pounds has been poured as this increasingly popular sport develops.

Grantown brings us to the fringe of the Cairngorms, the splendid mountains fringed with old pine forests and diversified by small lochs, which form the centre of the Grampians.

From Grantown up to Newtonmore the upper Spey carries a deep valley which is followed both by the main road, one of General Wade's, and by the railway, which offers the readiest access to these splendid mountains. Consequently, the length of Speyside is strung with highland resorts.

The chief of these, Kingussie, the capital of Badenoch, is an old village which took its present form when it was replanned as a woollen centre by the Duke of Gordon towards the close of the eighteenth century. Kingussie now has a famous Highland Folk Museum, founded by Dr. I. F. Grant. The Ruthven Barracks were the site both of high hopes and of despair at the time of the '45. They were successfully captured by the Jacobite army during the early part of the campaign: they were also the point at which the clans rallied after Culloden to be finally dispersed by the discomfited Prince Charles Edward.

The Cairngorms are the highest mountain range in Britain, though no individual peak reaches the height of Ben Nevis in the west. The four main peaks are Ben Macdhui (4,296 feet), Braeriach (4,248 feet), Cairn Toul (4,241 feet), and Cairngorm (4,084 feet) and there are several other points or full summits topping 4,000 feet. The range forms the most impressive part of the wide stretch of mountains in western Aberdeenshire, Inverness-shire and Perthshire which is known collectively as the Grampians, a name deriving from the sixteenth century chronicler, Hector Boece, who adopted Tacitus's "Mons Grampius."

The Cairngorms, like Ben Nevis, are a granite formation, and they yield semi-precious stones, known as "cairngorms", transparent crystals of smoked quartz with beautiful colouring, which are often worked into brooches of silver or set in the end of a grouse claw.

The corries and cliffs of the area have long been famous for their rock and ice-climbing, but all the mountains have accessible, if laborious, easy ascents. Some of the sting can be taken out of these by using ponies and the area has recently seen a great increase in pony-trekking which was first developed in its modern form at Newtonmore.

Since the Second World War the major sporting development in the Cairngorms has been the growth of ski-ing. So far as Britain is concerned this used to be a sport of the privileged few who could afford protracted winter sports holidays in Switzerland, Austria or Norway. Then suddenly, the ski-slopes on Scottish mountains were "discovered" and exploited.

All the tourist resorts along Speyside have benefited from the boom in ski-ing, but the nearest resort to the ski-slopes is Aviemore, a village which was a product of the railway in the nineteenth century. From there a good road now leads past Coylumbridge and Loch Morlich up to Glen More from which a 2½-mile "ski-road" climbs the shoulder of Cairngorms to the ski-lifts. Beyond that is a chair lift going right up on to the summit slopes. As fast as new facilities of this kind are provided, they are overtaxed, and the whole area is being intensively developed.

Glen More, with the beautiful Loch Morlich, provides an excellent centre. There are no hotels there, and planning permission would not be given to erect one, but the Scottish Council for Physical Recreation has a modern training centre, Glen More Lodge. In the summer this provides courses in rock-climbing, mountain-walking and dinghy-sailing on Loch Morlich. In the winter, tuition is given in both ski-ing and snow and ice-climbing. Before the making of the new road to Glen More, this centre was housed in the old Glen More Lodge, which now serves as a youth hostel.

Loch Morlich is 1,000 feet above sea level, and fringed with sandy beaches which descend to the water from forestland of old Scots pine; it has good sailing and swimming and is justly a tremendous attraction; though there are many who regret the quiet it used to enjoy before the road was driven through. The whole area has been affected in the same way. Even the White Lady Shieling high on the shoulder of Cairn Gorm, which used to be a rough bivouac hut for climbers and skiers, now has a restaurant.

Ski-ing is rapidly becoming one of the most popular sports in Scotland.

The Cairngorms, a mountain range of great variety and colour.

The Glen More National Forest Park extends for 12,500 acres around Loch Morlich, and the Nature Conservancy administers the 40,000 acre Cairngorms Nature Reserve, which is the largest of its kind in Britain and includes the summits of Braeriach and Cairn Toul.

The ancient Caledonian Forest of old pines suffered tremendously during the eighteenth and early nineteenth centuries from the coincidence of a high demand for timber, owing to smelting with charcoal, and a financial pressure felt by Highland landlords who aspired to take up the more spacious ways of the fashionable English aristocracy. The Forest Park contains some of the surviving remnants of ancient forest as well as modern afforestation.

In the Cairngorms Nature Reserve the summits of the mountains are of particular interest. As Fraser Darling and Morton Boyd have written: "The country of the summits is, in the Highlands, an immense archipelago of biological islands holding relict communities of a past age—that of the last post-glacial epoch."

The Reserve boasts golden eagles and ptarmigans, but the great event of the year for naturalists has been the return of the ospreys. The osprey, an eagle-like bird, which hunts over water, used to be common in the Highlands but was extinct by the beginning of this century. A pair appeared at Loch Garten in 1958, and, carefully guarded, have nested there since. Loch Garten has been made a statutory bird sanctuary to protect them.

Loch Garten, the beautiful wild home of the Ospreys.

The Lairig Ghru, dividing Inverness-shire from Aberdeenshire, a scenic pass on the headwaters of the Dee.

Below, The Linn of Dee, 6 miles from Braemar, spanned by Queen Victoria's bridge.

Considerable tracts of the Cairngorms, and in particular the southern slopes, are given over to grouse-moors and deer-forests, and access is restricted, especially during the stalking season. But there are two traditional rights of way which pass through the mountains: from Aviemore to Braemar by Loch Morlich and the Lairig Loaigh, and from Aviemore to Braemar by the Lairig Ghru, the greatest of the Cairngorm passes.

These routes lead over to the classic tourist area of Deeside. The River Dee, which has carved its course here, rises from the Wells of Dee high on the summit plateau of Braeriach, and from this snowy source flows 85 miles eastwards to Aberdeen. It is the most rapid river in Scotland and for the greater part of its course it tumbles tumultuously over a boulder-strewn bed. The prominent waterfall in Fuar Gharbh-choire, the corrie where the river descends from the summit of Braeriach, is followed by a series of falls as the river rapidly loses 2,000 feet of height in the short distance between its source and Glen Dee.

Towards the head of the public motor road is the famous Linn of Dee where the river rushes through a chasm whose rocky sides approach in places to within four feet of each other. The Linn is spanned by a bridge which was opened by Queen Victoria.

A little farther down the river at Inverey a rough track runs up the River Ey to a spot where there is a shallow cave just above the water in a deep chasm. It is known as "the Colonel's Bed", there being a tradition that Colonel John Farquharson lay in hiding there after the Battle of Killiecrankie.

A majestic stretch of river descends from Inverey to Braemar, the highest of the Deeside villages. Braemar is really a dual village — Auchindryne, on the left bank, traditionally Catholic, and Castleton, on the right bank, traditionally Protestant.

Braemar Castle, the seat of the Farquharsons of Invercauld, was built by the Earl of Mar in 1628, suffered a burning in 1689, and was leased to the War Office as a barracks for a period. Kindrochit Castle had its origins in a hunting lodge built in the fourteenth century, but it has long been a ruin and is now little more than foundations. It was here that the Earl of Mar raised the Jacobite standard in 1715 after a hunting party, which was in fact a council of the Jacobite gentry.

The famous Braemar Gathering, a meeting for Highland games, piping and dancing, was started in 1832 by local initiative and acquired its fame after Queen Victoria attended in 1848. Now the Royal Family is traditionally present, the Gathering being a local one for them since Balmoral Castle is less than ten miles away.

Balmoral Castle is not an official residence of the Queen, but a private home. The estate was bought by the Prince Consort in 1852 for £31,500 after he and Queen Victoria had leased it for four years. Sir Robert Gordon was the previous owner, and he had developed the estate and the deer forest. It was on his death that the Prince Consort bought it and erected the present castle, built of local granite in the Scottish baronial style to designs of William Smith, the city architect of Aberdeen, who was greatly influenced by discussions with the Prince.

Crathie Church dates from 1895 and is the work of Marshall MacKenzie, architect of part of Marischal College, Aberdeen.

Since Victoria's time Balmoral has always been a holiday castle for the royal family, where they can relax and enjoy a change from the formality of a royal engagement list. Often informality goes hand in hand with privacy, but the Castle can accommodate over a hundred people and the ballroom, sixty-eight feet long and twenty-five feet wide, has seen many colourful occasions.

In the little hamlet of Crathie nearby is the church at which the royal family worships when they are in residence at Balmoral. The gates of the church are a memorial to King George VI. The church itself contains monuments to members of the royal family and there is a memorial to Queen Victoria's famous servant, John Brown, in the churchyard.

Ballater was the terminus of the railway line from Aberdeen up Deeside, Queen Victoria having insisted that the rails should not be driven farther up to Balmoral.

The little town is a holiday resort in its own right, and its origin is amusing. Pannanich has wells and bogs and in 1760 a cure for scrofula was claimed for them. Colonel Francis Farquharson, when he returned from twenty years of exile after Culloden, publicised the cure, built an inn and created a spa which became fashionable.

Ballater bridge bears testimony to the power of the Dee. On it a plaque records the sweeping away of two stone bridges, one in 1789, and a second, built by Thomas Telford, in 1829. The present "Royal Bridge" was opened in 1885.

The 'Royal Bridge' at Ballater, a town which has seen many royal arrivals since 1848.

H

A contestant in the hammer-throwing at the Aboyne Games. The 'hammer' weighs 16 lbs.

Aboyne is justly famous for its Highland Games, which are held on an admirably level site close to the river every September on the day before the Braemar Gathering. The Aboyne Games are amongst the most serious and best of the Highland meetings and it was from here that reforms in the dress of girl dancers came. For many years girls in dancing competition wore an absurd short adaptation of male highland dress and hung themselves with medals. The whole effect was closer to a sentimental stage musical than to traditional country dancing. The "Aboyne Dress", a becoming adaptation of Scots peasant costume, is insisted upon by the Games Committee, and has spread in popularity.

The original village, Charleston of Aboyne, was the result of a charter granted to Charles Gordon, 1st Earl of Aboyne, for a burgh of barony close to Aboyne Castle. Present-day Aboyne, however, is mainly the late nineteenth-century foundation of Sir Cunliffe Brooks. It is an attractive village built round a green.

The last of the Deeside resorts as one descends the river is Banchory, only about 18 miles from Aberdeen. It is a thriving town, much of it terraced up the hillside, which stands close to the confluence of the Feugh and the Dee.

Banchory stands at a junction of ways. It lies on the main Deeside road, but gives access also to Stonehaven and the Mearns. The "Slug Road" to Stonehaven passes close to Raedykes, the main northernmost marching camp of the Romans, and offers magnificent views over the North Sea. The Cairn o' Mount road to Fettercairn and the Mearns climbs to almost 1500 feet, and was used by Macbeth, Edward I and Montrose.

The Town House, on the north side of Aberdeen's Union Street. Built in 1871, its turreted tower is 200 ft. high.

Aberdeen, which vies with Edinburgh for grace and interest, is really two cities, and markedly so. Dr. Johnson wrote of it in 1773:

"Old Aberdeen is the ancient episcopal city, in which are still to be seen the remains of the cathedral. It has the appearance of a town in decay, having been situated in times when commerce was yet unstudied, with very little attention to the commodities of the harbour.

"New Aberdeen has all the bustle of prosperous trade, and all the shew of increasing opulence. It is built by the water-side. The houses are large and lofty, and the streets spacious and clean. They build almost wholly with the granite used in the new pavement of the streets of London, which is well known not to want hardness, yet they shape it easily. It is beautiful and must be very lasting."

Save that Old Aberdeen is reviving from its decay, Johnson's description will still stand, though at the time he wrote, much of what is now the most impressive part of Aberdeen was not yet built.

The city lies between the two rivers, Dee and Don, New Aberdeen centred upon the Dee and Old Aberdeen upon the Don. The spine of New Aberdeen is the splendid Union Street, a broad thoroughfare a mile long. Although, like all shopping centres nowadays, it is somewhat marred by the clamour of modern shop-fronts, it is still a street of great restraint and dignity. Much of the original Regency work remains and, as Dr. Johnson remarked, the granite is not merely sparklingly beautiful but also so lasting that it might almost be newly built. The stone has scarcely weathered in two centuries.

The winter gloaming in Strath Don, Aberdeenshire.

The Castlegate, Aberdeen, still retains its beautiful seventeenth-century hexagonal Mercat Cross.

At the east end of Union Street, Castle Street runs into it and together they form the Castlegate, the square which is the traditional centre of New Aberdeen. It used to be an open market before modern traffic conditions made such an arrangement impossible.

At the east end of the modern municipal buildings is the square tower and spire of the Old Tolbooth, part of the seventeenth-century Town House. The North of Scotland Bank and the Athenaeum are both the work of Aberdeen's greatest architect, Archibald Simpson (1790-1847) amongst whose other works are the Music Hall, Bon Accord Square and Crescent, and the High School for Girls in Albyn Place. Nearby are two of the oldest houses in the city, Provost Ross's house in Shiprow, and Provost Skene's House.

Old Aberdeen lies to the north near a meander of the River Don, and is centred on the ancient Cathedral of St. Machar, a fine example of a fortified church and the only ancient cathedral of granite in Britain. In the main it is fifteenth-century work though the characteristic sandstone steeples on the twin west towers were added in the early sixteenth century by Bishop Gavin Dunbar.

The nave is still used for worship.

The best of Old Aberdeen, the High Street, Chanonry, Dunbar Street, Don Street and others, which contains many old houses, is being carefully restored and harmonised with university extensions. The Chanonry is particularly fine and contains in Chaplain's Court, which dates from 1519, the oldest inhabited house in Aberdeen.

The twin towers of St Machar's Cathedral, Old Aberdeen, an unusual wintry view.

117

The centre of the intellectual life of Aberdeen is the University, which was until as late as 1860 two separate universities. King's College, the older of the two, lies in Old Aberdeen and was founded in 1495 by Bishop Elphinstone. It is thus, after St. Andrews and Glasgow, the third oldest of the Scottish universities, and Hector Boece, the famous historian, was its first principal. The main survival of its older buildings is the chapel, which has a fine lantern tower. The Cromwell Tower is an old hall of residence, built partly from monies contributed by General Monk and Cromwell's officers. Many old houses in the area of King's College are coming into the hands of the university and are being restored.

The second university was Marischal College, founded in 1593 by George Keith, Earl Marischal, as a specifically Protestant foundation. Until the 1840's it occupied the old buildings of the Greyfriars Monastery. The main building now is in Broad Street in the New Town, a quadrangle with an elaborate facade in perpendicular Gothic designed by Marshall Mackenzie and opened in 1906.

The two colleges, together with the medical school housed in the infirmary at Foresterhill, are now part of a single university. The medical school has long been in the forefront of gynaecological research and medical sociology and there are other important research institutes in the city, specializing in soil research, animal nutrition, fish preservation and fishing techniques.

As well as its university, Aberdeen has a college of education, an old fifteenth-century grammar school, at which Byron was educated, and the eighteenth-century Robert Gordon's College, a campus which includes a technical college, a school of art and a secondary school.

Aberdeen has a landward face and a seaward face. It is the metropolis for Deeside and for the rich farming areas to north and south, and it is often said that the Aberdonian is a countryman rather than a city man. The local hosiery industry and textile weaving are landward industries, as is the food-canning and sausage and pie-making. Granite-quarrying and polishing are a special feature of the place, as the great cliff of the huge Rubislaw quarry proclaims.

Other industries represent the seaward face of Aberdeen. Paper-making depends largely on the importation of wood-pulp from the Baltic. Cordage, tarpaulins and nets are manufactures that smack of shipping and fisheries and Aberdeen also has its shipyards.

Above all, of course, the city is one of Britain's greatest fishing centres, with a large trawler fleet. Fish auctions are held each morning at the bustling fish market beside the Albert Basin and hundreds of tons of fish change hands every day to be sent inland or south by road or rail. The fishing basins are only part of a larger artificial harbour, constructed under difficult conditions by Smeaton and Telford among others, and Aberdeen has an important trade with the Baltic and Scandinavia, as well as serving as the principal mainland port for Orkney and Shetland.

To those unfamiliar with Aberdeen perhaps the most surprising aspect of its seaward face is that it is Scotland's largest seaside resort, with golf courses, a swimming pool, a pleasure beach and dance halls. In Aberdeen the visitor can combine sea beaches and the Highland hinterland with all the activity and facilities which a large city can offer in cinemas and restaurants.

The fish market, Aberdeen. The auction takes place every day at 8 a.m.

Wild red deer in the Cairngorms

Indeed, Aberdeen with its two faces, Highland and seashore, might be taken to sum up Scotland as playground and tourist resort; and field sports and tourism have been important to the economic life of Scotland for a hundred years.

In the eighteenth century, when Boswell and Johnson visited Scotland, Highland scenery was not appreciated and the travellers looked upon the Highlands and islands as a kind of desert, imposing hardship on its inhabitants and its visitors. Sir Walter Scott may be said to have played the greatest part in changing attitudes to the wild and rugged part of Scotland, and in the nineteenth century painters popularized a romantic view of mountain and moorland, stags and Highland cattle.

It was the development of the railways which made Scotland accessible and the influence of Queen Victoria and a Leicester businessman called Thomas Cook that made Scotland a popular resort.

The purchase of Balmoral by the Queen and Prince Albert made Scotland fashionable and during the nineteenth century the aristocracy and prosperous classes came north to their shooting lodges for deerstalking, fishing and the sport of the grouse moors. Although the sport provided jobs for some, it was disadvantageous in national terms since it led to the clearance of crofters from their lands to render inviolable the huge sporting estates of great landowners.

More certain in its economic advantages was the tourism organized by Thomas Cook, founder of the world famous travel agency, who built his business on Scottish tours for the middle classes. His tours started in the 1840's and by the 1860's he had built up to a substantial traffic and even published a guide, *Cook's Scottish Tourist*.

121

Immediately to the south of Aberdeen lies one
of Scotland's smallest counties,
Kincardineshire, often known simply as "the
Mearns." The town of Kincardine has long
disappeared, never having been more than a
cluster of cottages built round a former royal
castle, which was demolished in the mid-
seventeenth century. But although this
tangible monument has been erazed, the
Howe o' the Mearns, the fertile inland
farming area of the county which centres on
the site of the ruins remains one of those
districts in which history lies deep-rooted in
the dialect and customs of the people.

One of Scotland's greatest modern novelists,
Lewis Grassic Gibbon, set his finest novel,
Sunset Song, in the Mearns and, in describing
the passing away of the old rural values and
customs during the First World War,
provided a memorial of them rather as
Hardy did for Wessex.

The chief town of the Howe o' the Mearns
is Laurencekirk, which was founded in its
modern shape by Francis Garden, an
eighteenth-century sheriff of Mearns, who
became Lord Gardenstone and a Court of
Session judge. Garden bought the estate of
Johnston and encouraged the planned
expansion of Laurencekirk, introducing
handloom weaving and snuffbox-making as
local industries. Boswell, who visited
Laurencekirk on his tour with Johnson,
commented: "Lord Gardenstone is the
proprietor of Laurence Kirk, and has
encouraged the building of a manufacturing
village, of which he is exceedingly fond, and
has written a pamphlet upon it, as if he had
founded Thebes." They stayed at the
Gardenstone Arms, which Lord Gardenstone
had furnished with a library "that travellers
might have entertainment for the mind", but
Johnson "wished there had been more books,
and those better chosen."

Muchalls is the queen of the coast, a cliff-top village with its own castle. The castle, which dates from the seventeenth century, has a variety of features to attract the romantic disposition. Although the smugglers' passage to Gin Shore was sealed at the end of the nineteenth century and is now lost, there is a secret staircase within the castle, a wishing well in the courtyard and as genuine a ghost as any castle can claim. The great hall has a superbly delicate and elaborate plaster ceiling, and a magnificent overmantel, and other rooms have similar decorations only a little less splendid. The coastline of this part is perhaps the most sensational in Scotland and sets off both village and castle.

Muchalls Castle, built 1619-27, contains spectacular plasterwork and a collection of antiques.

The pleasant village of Fettercairn, though it might seem to claim its fame from an incognito visit of Queen Victoria and Prince Albert, which is pretentiously commemorated by a royal arch, is more renowned now for its associations with Boswell. Fettercairn House, erected in the second half of the seventeenth century by John, First Earl of Middleton, later passed to a Miss Stuart who married Sir William Forbes, Boswell's executor. Forbes brought a collection of Boswell's letters and journals to Fettercairn where they lay until they were discovered in the present century, purchased by Yale University, and quite recently published.

The most attractive villages of Kincardineshire are probably those small fishing communities which rest on its rocky coast and are now greatly in decline. Portlethen, Downies and Newtonhill have attracted people who work in Aberdeen. Findon, from which the name "finnan" haddock is derived, no longer smokes fish over peat cottage fires, but still attracts artists and tourists.

Stonehaven is caught within a deeply scooped bay into which runs the Cowie water and the Caron water.

Stonehaven has been the county town since the decline of Kincardine in the mid-seventeenth century. To the southern end of the town the old Quarter clusters round the interesting harbour which still has a much-diminished fishing industry alongside an increasing number of pleasure craft. To the north beyond the Cowie Water lies the old village of Cowie.

The new town, terraced up the hill above a central square, joins the two old villages together and contains the administrative offices of the county. But history clusters round the harbour, and particularly in the old Tolbooth, in which episcopal ministers were imprisoned and from which they christened children through the bars of their cell.

Two miles south of Stonehaven stands Dunnottar Castle. The rock was once an ancient Pictish stronghold, and its approach through a ravine known as St. Ninian's Den hints at early Christian associations. An early fortress was stormed by William Wallace in 1297 when held by the English, but the castle whose ruins now survive dates from a fourteenth-century keep built by Sir William Keith, Great Marischal of Scotland.

Dunnottar was the last stronghold of the Scottish Royalists in the Civil War, and in 1652 was subjected to an eight-month siege, which ended in surrender only after Charles II's private papers had been smuggled out sewn into a woman's clothing and the Scottish Crown jewels had been successfully hidden beneath the pulpit at Kinneff.

Dunnottar Castle stands on a rocky headland jutting from ranges of cliffs.

The continuation of the Howe o' the Mearns
south-westward into Angus is the great fertile
valley between the south-eastern fringe of the
Highlands and the Sidlaw Hills, the heart of
Strathmore.

Just over the border from Kincardineshire,
near the North Esk, lies the neat village of
Edzell with its broad main street, an inland
tourist resort, replanned in the nineteenth
century but dating originally from the
sixteenth. The ruined castle, whose well-
preserved Stirling Tower dates from the same
period, was once the gracious home of the
Lindsays of Glenesk.

Brechin, which stands on the South Esk, is
an ancient red sandstone town, which now
serves as the centre for a rich farming district.
Its cathedral is now a parish church, though the
title of Bishop of Brechin is still maintained
in the Episcopalian church. The building in
parts goes back to the thirteenth century, but
it suffered an indiscriminate restoration in the
early nineteenth century. Most interesting is
the unusual round-tower over 80 feet high
and only 15 feet in diameter at the base. It is
an example of a style of Celtic tower rare in
Scotland and typical of Ireland.

Brechin was the scene of a dismal episode
in Scottish history. It was here that John
Balliol, "the Toom Tabard", resigned the
realm of Scotland to the Bishop of Durham,
the agent of Edward I of England. Edward
made a triumphal progress through Scotland,
as far north as Elgin, and carried off to
England the so-called "Coronation Stone"
of the Scottish kings, securing such a grip on
Scotland that it took all the efforts of William
Wallace and Robert the Bruce to re-establish
the independence of the northern kingdom.

The county town of Angus, which was formerly called Forfarshire, is the little royal burgh of Forfar. Founded on textiles, particularly jute and linen, Forfar has little to distinguish it from the other small towns of the area except perhaps the confectionery known as Forfar rock and the type of meat pasty called in Scotland a Forfar bridie.

In the past, however, the town was notorious for the ruthless energy with which it pursued witches. A large number were burnt here in the seventeenth century and the Town Hall retains a metal bridle and gag as a memorial to bygone brutality.

The countryside around is rich in archaeological remains. On Turin Hill, north-east of the town, is Kemp Castle, probably one of the oldest stone forts in Scotland. Southwards at Tealing is an iron age souterrain or earth-house in a good state of preservation, and at Aberlemno there are Pictish sculptured stones.

Kirriemuir is Forfar's sister town, only six miles away and also heavily dependent on the jute industry. Kirriemuir was one of the last towns in Scotland to abandon the handloom, and was famous for its weavers. Hence J. M. Barrie called it "Thrums", the name for the unwoven ends of the warp threads left on the loom when the cloth is removed.

The author of *Peter Pan* was born in the town and his birthplace, a small house on the Brechin Road, is now kept as a personal museum. The "Auld Licht Manse" of the Little Minister lies across the road and the "Window in Thrums" is still to be seen at the top of the brae above the mill, at the other end of the town.

Glamis Castle, childhood home of Queen Elizabeth the Queen Mother, youngest daughter of the 14th Earl of Strathmore and Kinghorne.

Glamis is a name to conjure with, largely because of the unhistorical connection with Shakespeare's Macbeth, an association given resonance by the fact that Malcolm II died in the neighbourhood, according to some accounts, by foul play.

The present castle is mainly seventeenth-century work though parts of the tower are much older. The castle was forfeited to the Crown in 1537 when Lady Glamis was burned for witchcraft, but later restored to the Lyon family, one of whom, Patrick Lyon, became Earl of Strathmore in 1677. It was he who built the main parts of the present castle, which remains in the family. Queen Elizabeth, the Queen Mother, spent much of her childhood at Glamis and Princess Margaret was born in the castle in 1930.

From Strathmore there run up into the south-eastern fringes of the Highlands the Angus Glens, Glen Esk, Glen Clova, Glen Prosen and Glen Isla. The exceptional charm of these glens is enhanced by the fact that they are not overrun by tourists, probably because all except Glen Isla have roads which lead to no outlet.

Glen Esk runs down from Loch Lee to Edzell, carved by the course of the North Esk which for much of the way is delightfully wooded. At the Retreat, between the village of Tarfside and the foot of the glen, is a small but interesting folk museum. Prosen has a memorial fountain to the Antarctic explorers, Scott and Wilson, who knew and loved the glen. Glen Isla, like Glen Clova, is noted for its rare plants.

Glen Prosen under snow, one of the Angus glens that strike up into the hills from Kirriemuir.

I

Left, the ski lift at Glenshee, running from the top of the Devil's Elbow.

Bottom, Dunkeld Cathedral on the north bank of the Tay. The restored Choir is used as a parish church.

Glenshee is the most easterly of the Perthshire glens. It strikes deep into the mountains and carries the main road north from Perth to Deeside over the Cairnwell Pass, the highest main road, in Britain reaching 2,199 feet at the summit of the pass between Glas Maol and Cairnwell. The route was originally an eighteenth-century military road, and for the most part keeps its old line though there have been improvements at the Devil's Elbow, a series of steep hairpin turns near the summit.

The Cairnwell road is usually the first main road in Scotland to be blocked by snow, and with this natural advantage, the upper part of Glenshee has become a ski resort which rivals Glencoe and the Cairngorms. Glenshee is generally the most accessible of the three. Right up to Blairgowrie the route from Edinburgh, Dundee, Glasgow and the Midland industrial belt, is entirely on fast main roads, and one cannot drive anywhere between Stirling and Perth on a winter week-end without being aware of the busy traffic of cars bearing skis on their roof-racks. Not surprisingly there is a considerable problem in parking up the narrow Glenshee road when the verges are snowed up.

All the hotels in the area are booked up all winter, and the old Spittal hotel, which was burnt down in 1958, has been rebuilt in the style of the Scandinavian tourist hotels in the ski resorts. There is a chairlift on Cairnwell and several ski-tows in the area. Like all the ski resorts, Glenshee is becoming fashionable and even the little Strathmore towns of Alyth and Blairgowrie are feeling the boom.

Right, the main street of Pitlochry, part of General Wade's road across the Grampians to Inverness.

Bottom, Pitlochry dam, with the salmon ladder in the foreground.

The other main road north from Perth is that which follows first the course of the Tay and then that of the Garry up to the Pass of Drumochter and down into the valley of the Spey.

Dunkeld, an ancient cathedral city with fewer than a thousand inhabitants, is the gateway to this route. The cathedral, built in the fourteenth and fifteenth centuries, was the crown of an ecclesiastical tradition which goes back to an eighth-century monastery. The completed cathedral stood for less than a century before it was reduced to a roofless but still majestic ruin in the uncontrolled enthusiasm of the Reformation. Much of the historic atmosphere of the town remains and the National Trust for Scotland has taken an interest in the preservation of the old houses. Dunkeld is beautifully set on the salmon-rich Tay, spanned by a fine Telford bridge, and the wooded hills around make it a most attractive resort.

Pitlochry, thirteen miles on up the Tummel, is yet more famous as a highland resort, and claims to be the centre of Scotland. The town is thronged with hotels and a summer season of plays is offered at the Pitlochry Festival Theatre. The fishing is classic, and the surrounding hills and mountains offer both gentle woodland walks and strenuous climbing.

Pitlochry is also an important element in the Tummel-Garry hydro-electric scheme, and this has created an additional and unusual tourist attraction. In order to maintain the run of salmon up the river to their spawning grounds the dam at Pitlochry has been by-passed by a fish-ladder of artificially created pools with observation windows so that visitors can watch the fish passing up or down river.

Loch Faskally, an artificially created lake resulting from the Tummel-Garry hydro-electric scheme, is a welcome addition to the beauty of the district.

This dam has materially changed the landscape of the neighbourhood by creating a new loch in the Tummel valley. At the time the scheme was planned, there was a great deal of opposition to this intrusion on nature, but the operation has been conducted with tact, and however much the old familiars of Pitlochry may mourn the change, in the eyes of the visitor the new loch, Loch Faskally, is a beauty spot of the district.

Immediately north of Pitlochry the main road follows the Garry north westwards along the fringes of the Forest of Atholl. Atholl is the wild and mountainous north-eastern area of Perthshire, which contributed its name to the unusual drink, Atholl Brose, a rich and warming mixture of whisky, honey and oatmeal.

The road and railway both follow the Pass of Killiecrankie beside the River Garry.

Here was fought the glorious and tragic Battle of Killiecrankie. When, in the Constitutional Revolution of 1688, Parliament offered the throne to William and Mary, Claverhouse, Viscount Dundee, was commissioned to raise the clans in the Jacobite cause. General Mackay's army was attacked by 3,000 barefoot Highlanders above the Haugh of Urrard north of the pass. The government forces were routed and in the words of Macaulay, "the mingled torrent of red coats and tartans went raving down the valley to the gorge of Killiecrankie." The Soldier's Leap is an astonishing jump said to have been cleared by one of Mackay's soldiers in flight from the Highlanders.

The Vale of Atholl at the historic battle scene of Killiecrankie.

Although redesigned in 1745 and given extra castellation (1869), Blair Castle still shows traces of its original plan. Inside there are collections of paintings, porcelain, natural objects, furniture and embroidery. It is said to be the last British castle to have withstood a siege.

Blair Atholl, above the Pass, is a holiday centre at the outlet of Glen Tilt into Glen Garry. Close by Blair Atholl village lies the seat of the Duke of Atholl, Blair Castle. The earldom has been in one family from the fifteenth century, though it passed through the female line in the seventeenth. The oldest part of the castle, Comyn's Tower, was probably built by John Comyn of Badenoch in the thirteenth century. Later Blair Castle was a haven of Jacobitism. Montrose and Claverhouse both garrisoned it and Claverhouse's body was brought to Blair after Killiecrankie. Prince Charles Edward also stayed at Blair in 1745.

A little way up the road from Blair Castle is the picturesque Bruar Water with the Falls of Bruar. The woodland surrounding the falls is amusingly associated with Burns, who dedicated to the Duke of Atholl his *Humble Petition of Bruar Water*, a plea to the Duke to plant trees to shade the river. After complaining of the sun wasting its waters and scorching its trout, Bruar Water pleads:

Last day I grat wi' spite and teen,
  As Poet Burns came by,
That, to a Bard, I should be seen
  Wi' half my channel dry;
A panegyric rhyme, I ween,
  Ev'n as I was, he shar'd me;
But had I in my glory been,
  He, kneeling, wad ador'd me.
Would, then, my noblest master please
  To grant my highest wishes,
He'll shade my banks wi' tow'ring trees,
  And bonie spreading bushes.
Delighted doubly then, my lord,
  You'll wander on my banks,
And listen monie a grateful bird
  Return you tuneful thanks.

What landed proprietor could resist the plea of so articulate a stream!

Beyond the famous salmon leap at the falls of Garry is Struan, the site of the ancient burial ground of the Robertsons, another faithful Jacobite family which gave staunch support to the Stuart dynasty from the Civil Wars right up to the '45. Glen Errochty, which strikes westwards here, is the very heart of the Robertson country.

Dalnaspidal, which lies just below the summit of the Drumochter Pass, is the last village on the southern side of the watershed and boasts the highest railway station in Scotland. Close by is the Wade Stone, erected when the original road over the pass was built by the famous military road builder, General Wade, in 1728-9. The road was modernised later by Thomas Telford, and is thus associated with both of the greatest of Scotland's road builders, men who between them were more than any others responsible for laying the foundations of internal travel in this difficult country.

On the watershed to the east of Dalnaspidal is the highest point of the great Tummel Valley hydro-electric scheme where an intake weir and tunnel diverts water from the Edendon Water to Loch an Duin. The loch, which is in fact north of the watershed and has been made to outflow southwards through a tunnel, is 1,574 feet above sea level and between it and the Pitlochry Dam, on the River Tummel, at the lower end of the scheme there is all the power of a fall of 1,150 feet to be harnessed. Much of the water produces electricity at four or five power stations on its way down the valley. In the whole scheme there are nine power stations, harnessing rainfall from a catchment area of 710 square miles.

Field Marshal George Wade (1673-1748). In 1724 he was sent to the Highlands to construct a system of metalled roads. The project, which included building 40 remarkable stone bridges, was completed by 1730.

Below, Thomas Telford (1757-1834). Born near Westernick in Dumfriesshire, he was employed by the government in 1803 on a Highlands development project which included the construction of the Caledonian canal and 900 miles of road.

The "Road to the Isles" lies through this magnificent glen, then along Loch Rannoch (left) to Rannoch Station.

Western Perthshire is dominated by four great valleys running roughly east and west. The most northerly is that which is marked by Loch Tummel and Loch Rannoch, next is Glen Lyon, third is Loch Tay and Glen Dochart and the smallest and most southerly is the line of Loch Earn and Loch Voil.

The most northerly and least promising of these routes is that of the "Road to the Isles":

*By Tummel and Loch Rannoch and Lochaber
I will go.*

There is no modern motor road through but the drive from Killiecrankie to the station of Rannoch on the West Highland Railway is in its way one of the finest in Scotland. Queen's View, from a rocky spur close to the road above Loch Tummel, commands a prospect of the loch with the characteristic shape of Schichallion, a perfect cone, behind.

The western end of the loch is bare and wild as is the stretch of country between Tummel Bridge and Kinloch Rannoch at the eastern end of Loch Rannoch, where the River Tummel flows out of the loch. It is a clean, trim village which celebrates with a memorial "the Rannoch Schoolmaster, Evangelist, and Sacred Poet", Dugald Buchanan, a Gaelic writer and one of the past breed of Scottish dominies.

Loch Rannoch itself is 10 miles long and a mile wide, splendidly set with views to the west across the Moor of Rannoch to the Glencoe mountains. Near Dall on the south shore is a preserved remnant of old Caledonian pines from the fringe of the Black Wood of Rannoch. Beyond the loch all is desolation except for the oddly incongruous Rannoch Station beyond which stretches the waste of the Moor.

Below, Prince Charles Edward Stuart, "Bonny Prince Charlie" (1720-88). Born and educated in Rome, he returned there after more than twenty years of wandering disguised around Europe. This portrait by Maurice Quentin de la Tour was painted shortly after the flight to France in 1746.

The Tummel flows into the Tay between Dunkeld and Pitlochry, and from this point Strathtay stretches away to the west to the loch. The road, which follows the valley to Aberfeldy and Kenmore, branches off the main Drumochter road at the pleasing little village of Ballinluig, whose slender claim to fame is that its inn, like many others, was visited by Bonnie Prince Charlie.

North of the confluence, the road crosses the Tummel to the village of Logierait. This was once the site of the Regality court of the Lords of Atholl, said to have been over seventy feet long, but now entirely effaced. Some traces of the prison remain in the yard of the inn and a carved nineteenth-century cross in memory of the 6th Duke of Atholl stands on the former hanging knoll. Rob Roy Macgregor escaped from the prison within a day of his lodgement there, and in 1745 six hundred prisoners, taken by the Jacobite army at Prestonpans, were housed there. The churchyard has three heavy iron mortsafes intended as protection against body-snatchers.

Grandtully Castle, a few miles up the Strath, has been the seat of the Stuarts of Grandtully since the fourteenth century, though the present castle is mainly sixteenth-century in foundation. The upper part of the building was radically remodelled in 1626 by the Sheriff of Perth of that time, Sir William Stuart, and his wife Agnes Moncrieff, and later extensions were made in the nineteenth century. The castle stands in a splendid park and nearby it is the old church of St. Mary, now disused and part of a farm steading, but formerly the traditional burial ground of the Stuarts of Grandtully.

Below, the Crieff road into Aberfeldy, well-known as a holiday centre.

Bottom, Castle Menzies, near Weem. The original building dates from the late 16th century, but 19th-century additions were made.

The queen of the upper Tay valley is the little Highland town of Aberfeldy, whose pride is the finest of all General Wade's bridges, the Tay Bridge, built in 1733. At the southern end of the bridge a cairn erected in 1887 commemorates the enrolment in 1740 of the Frecadan Dubh or Black Watch, 42nd regiment of the line. The regiment had its origin in "the Watch" raised in 1667 by Whig clan chiefs to keep watch over the Highlands. The men wore a dark tartan with a green base which distinguished them from the Red Soldiers, as the guardsmen were called, and it is from this dark clothing that the name, "Black Watch" derived.

General Wade, when he was building his road and the bridge at Aberfeldy, reputedly stayed at the inn in the nearby village of Weem and the oldest part of the present hotel is said to date from 1527. The old church at Weem, no longer used for services, dates from the sixteenth century in its present form, though its foundation goes back to at least the first half of the thirteenth century, when it is mentioned in charters. It has been used since 1839 as a mausoleum for the Menzies family. The church also contains two of three "girth-crosses" which marked a sanctuary enclosure at the Culdee Celtic monastery of Dull. The third cross remains in Dull village. Another ancient religious memorial nearby is St. David's Well and cave up on the steep face of Weem Rock. Castle Menzies, close by the village, is a sixteenth-century Scottish mansion, extended in the nineteenth century and now maintained by the Clan Menzies Society as a clan centre.

139

*The village of
Kenmore whose
planned beauty was
praised in a hasty
poem by Burns.*

Kenmore, at the foot of Loch Tay, is a pleasant "model village", replanned by the 3rd Earl of Breadalbane in 1760. The River Tay is born as the outflow from the loch and at Kenmore is its highest bridge, built in 1774. Burns visited the village, greatly admired the view from the bridge, and wrote "with a pencil over the chimney-piece, in the parlour of the inn at Kenmore" a poem in praise of the beauty of the district:

The meeting cliffs each deep-sunk glen divides:
The woods, wild-scatter'd, clothe their ample sides;
Th' outstretching lake, inbosomed 'mong the hills,
The eye with wonder and amazement fills:
The Tay meand'ring sweet in infant pride,
The palace rising on his verdant side,
The lawns wood-fring'd in Nature's native taste,
The hillocks dropt in Nature's careless haste....

The palace on the verdant bank was no doubt Balloch Castle, built in the sixteenth century by Grey Colin, 3rd Laird of Glenorchy. It has gone for ever, replaced in the nineteenth century by the extravagantly lavish Taymouth Castle. It was here that the capercailzie, having died out in Scotland, was reintroduced from Swedish stock by the Earl of Breadalbane in the mid-nineteenth century.

Loch Tay itself dominates the scene. Fifteen miles long and a mile broad it is famous for its salmon fishing. There are several islands in the loch; a causeway, now submerged, joined one of the islands to the mainland and Sybilla, wife of Alexander I, is said to have died and been buried here. Spey Island is an artificial island, though probably prehistoric in origin.

Loch Tay, its glassy waters rich in salmon and islands.

141

Left, the River Dochart near Killin.

Bottom, sowing by hand in the Killin area.

The northern bank of the loch is dominated by Ben Lawers, at 3,984 feet the highest mountain in Perthshire. Much of its southern slopes, which are rich in rare alpine plants, are owned by the National Trust for Scotland. From the summit on a clear day both western and eastern coasts of Scotland are visible.

The northern shore of the loch is also unusually rich in prehistoric remains including frequent cup-and-ring markings and a bronze-age burial site marked by a circle of standing stones.

At the head of Loch Tay is the tourist village of Killin, a place attractive rather for its situation than for any distinction of building or planning. Ben Lawers towers above it. Loch Tay stretches eastwards. The River Dochart runs a splendid series of falls and rapids through the village, spanned by an adventurous road bridge, to be joined below the village by the River Lochay.

Just below the bridge is a small wooded island which is the traditional burial place of the Clan MacNab; and the former seat of the MacNabs, Kinnell House, is on the southern bank of the river opposite the village. Kinnell House subsequently passed to the Breadalbane family, and the 2nd Marquess planted a famous and fruitful black vine. Among the more ancient monuments of the district are the standing stone circle in the grounds of Kinnell House and the eight healing stones of St. Fillan, each having healing powers over the part of the body whose shape it resembles.

Glen Lochray, just to the north of Killin, is a favourite walking place for visitors who seem to have found added interest rather than a deterrent in the tactfully executed hydro-electric works.

Immediately to the north of Loch Tay, on the road from Aberfeldy and Weem to Glen Lyon, are the two villages of Coshieville and Fortingall.

Coshieville is a small hamlet and inn on one of the main drove routes along which cattle were brought to the markets of Falkirk and Crieff. It stands at a meeting place of routes from Rannoch, Glen Lyon, Loch Tay and Aberfeldy.

Nearby the formidable Garth Castle stands above the ravine of the Keltney Burn. This was formerly a stronghold of the "Wolf of Badenoch." Also in the neighbourhood is the ruin of Comrie Castle, dating from the fourteenth century, which was formerly the seat of the Menzies clan before Castle Menzies, near Aberfeldy, took its place. Fortingall is a planned "model village" with a well-known inn, which was built towards the end of the nineteenth century by Sir Donald Currie, who bought Glen Lyon House, once a stronghold of the Campbells, together with the estate. He not only planned the village but rebuilt the mansion house.

Fortingall boasts a yew-tree in the churchyard claimed to be between 2,000 and 3,000 years old. According to a report of Pennant in the second half of the eighteenth century the girth of the tree was then over 56 feet, and it still survives. Fortingall's other main claim to fame is the story that Pontius Pilate was born there, his father a Roman legionary involved in the occupation of Britain and his mother either a Menzies or a MacLaren. But the nearby "Roman fort" is probably a relic of early medieval times. There are, however, many witnesses to early occupation in Bronze Age and Iron Age sites in the neighbourhood.

The village of Fortingall flanked by Drummond Hill which stands between it and Loch Tay to the south.

Glen Lyon, where forests of Caledonian pine and birch alternate with prosperous farmland.

Glen Lyon, whose Gaelic name is *Cromghleann nan clach*, "the crooked glen of the stones", is the longest true glen in Scotland. At the head of the glen, Loch Lyon has been considerably increased in size by damming and the water feeds the power station in Glen Lochay above Killin. The glen is rich in Iron Age settlements which old legends associated with Fionn's castles.

About half way down the glen at Bridge of Balgie a secondary road climbs over the shoulder of Ben Lawers to Loch Tay and from this a side road leads to a 1,400 foot high car park from which the ski slopes can be reached. From Bridge of Balgie downwards the glen gradually narrows and, at the entrance to the glen, woods and precipices intermingle on the steep sides.

144

South of Glen Lyon and Strathtay lies the other great valley of Perthshire, Strathearn, the centre of Perthshire farming.

Crieff lies at the midpoint of this valley, built on a hillside above the river. The town is a tourist centre and one of several dubbed "The Gateway to the Highlands," the road north from Crieff running through the well-known Sma' Glen.

The town was originally called Drummond, and the Drummonds, Dukes of Perth, have always been influential in its history, rebuilding it after it was burnt by the Jacobites in 1715, and earlier, in 1672, securing by Act of Parliament the establishment of its famous Tryst or annual cattle market, the centre of droving in Scotland until 1770 when Stenhousemuir became more important.

Crieff. The formal flowerbeds of the park look across the valley of Strathearn to the distant hills.

K

Gleneagles Hotel, seen across one of its three golf courses (including the 'Wee' which is nine holes).

Eastwards from Crieff the broad farming country stretches down to Perth with a fringe of mountains to the north always making their presence felt. The valley itself is satisfyingly undulating with upland stretches of gorse and water meadows down beside the river. The towns and villages are trim and prosperous. The main road from Perth to Stirling which runs through the lower part of Strathearn is one of the pleasantest of Scotland's midland trunk roads.

To the south-east of Crieff it passes through the royal burgh of Auchterarder, a long town strung along the road, with the remains of an ancient royal hunting castle. The town used to be a centre of hand-loom weaving and is still famous for woollen goods and tartans, though these are now factory-made.

Between Auchterarder and Blackford,

which has a historic brewing industry dating from the fifteenth century, is one of Scotland's most famous hotels, Gleneagles. This huge and lavish tourist hotel which belongs to British Rail, was built in the early 1920's by the old London, Midland and Scottish Railway Company, and was opened in 1923. From the attractive station an avenue of trees leads up to the hotel itself, built on the scale of the large city-centre railway hotels and surrounded by pleasant gardens. Attached to the hotel are two classic golf-courses, the King's Course, and the Queen's Course, planned by the famous Scottish golfer, James Braid, and maintained in superb condition. Gleneagles Hotel, with its swimming pool and large ballroom, its lawns and groves and golf courses, represents in the hotel trade the pattern of the tourist hotel, rather as the great Cunarders epitomize the tradition of the ocean liner.

Farther down the Earn valley are the two villages of Dunning and Forteviot, nestling under the eastern end of the Ochils.

Dunning is a large village, which has been left aside from modern development in a fold of the hills. In its closely-clustered plan it is quite unlike the typically strung-out villages on either side of the Ochils and is reminiscent of some of the English villages. The church has a very fine early thirteenth-century tower and in the centre of the village there is a thorn tree planted to commemorate the burning of Dunning by the Earl of Mar's soldiers after Sheriffmuir.

Forteviot spans the length of Scottish history. In early times it was the capital of the Pictish kingdom of Fortrenn. Kenneth MacAlpine died here in 860, and in medieval times there was a royal residence, now obliterated, just outside the present village.

To the north lies Methven, where Robert the Bruce, after being crowned on 25th March, 1306, and excommunicated by the Pope on 18th May, suffered a severe defeat by English forces on 19th June.

The religious tradition of Forteviot goes back to the Celtic Church, and there are two fine Celtic crosses surviving as well as an unusual Celtic church hand-bell. There is also the remains of a large Roman camp nearby.

In spite of all this historical association, the present village is not itself old. It falls within the estate which Sir John Dewar, the Perth distiller, bought from the Earl of Kinnoull just before the First World War. In 1925 Sir John's son, Lord Forteviot, demolished the old village and replaced it with a new model village planned by himself.

I. Taylor Sculp.

ROBERT BRUCE.

Loch Earn is graced by the villages of St. Fillans and Lochearnhead at its eastern and western ends.

In contrast to the broad agricultural valley east of Crieff, upper Strathearn from Crieff to the head of Loch Earn is Highland in character. Comrie, which is on the road between Crieff and the loch, lies exactly on the highland fault and has in the past been subject to minor earthquakes. The little town is a typical Highland centre with walking and pony-trekking in attractive country.

Loch Earn itself is pleasingly beautiful rather than dramatic, in spite of the impressive height of Ben Vorlich towering above its southern shore. The villages at either end of the loch, are well provided with good hotels and the loch has become a centre for sailing and water ski-ing. Loch Earn is of all Scottish lochs most reminiscent of the English Lakes.

Behind Lochearnhead there rises the eastern spur of a ridge of mountains which runs westwards to the head of Loch Lomond. To the north lie Glen Dochart above Killin and Glen Falloch above Ardlui, the two meeting at Crianlarich. To the east lies Glen Ogle on whose steep and boulder-strewn slopes the Callander and Oban railway line nearly foundered. To the south is Loch Voil and the notorious Braes of Balquhidder.

Caught within this close rectangle, the range of mountains, which culminates in the twin peaks of Ben More and Stobinian, is cut by deep corries carved by northward or southward running streams. The rough and furrowed mountains offer strenuous hill-walking which is compensated on the high peaks by superb views.

Ben More, a splendid peak in a deeply carved and fragmented ridge.

149

The Braes of
Balquhidder, once
the domain of Rob
Roy MacGregor.
Loch Voil, long and
narrow in the steep
valley, contains
salmon, trout and
char.

Rob Roy
(1671-1734), an
engraving after
an unknown
painting.

The Braes of Balquhidder beside Loch Voil
are famous for their beauty and their historical
associations. The bank of Loch Voil is rocky
and wooded with here and there a tiny shingle
beach and the loch itself is rich in salmon,
trout and char. The upper glen is wild and
trackless.

The troubled history of Balquhidder is
well characterised by Robert Louis Stevenson
in *Kidnapped*:

"No great clan held rule there; it was filled
and disputed by small septs and broken
remnants, and what they call 'chiefless folk,'
driven into the wild country about the
springs of Forth and Teith by the advance of
the Campbells. Here were Stewarts and
Maclarens . . . Here, too, were many of that
old proscribed, nameless, red-headed clan of
the MacGregors. They had always been
ill-considered, and now worse than ever,
having credit with no side or party in the
whole country of Scotland."

The MacGregor dominance culminated
in the exile there of the outlawed Rob Roy
MacGregor, who lorded it over the area.
Stevenson describes the behaviour of his son
Robert Oig in the same light. "He came in
with a great show of civility, but like a man
among inferiors; took off his bonnet to Mrs.
Maclaren, but clapped it on his head again to
speak to Duncan . . ."

In the churchyard of Kirkton of
Balquhidder, the only village in the glen, is
the grave of Rob Roy, his widow, and
probably two of his sons. Rob Roy lived a
Robin Hood life as an outlaw after his lands
had been seized for debt and his wife and
children turned out in midwinter; but he
died peacefully in his own house a few days
after Christmas in 1734.

Right, the River Leny at Strathyre. In this valley, Loch Lubnaig connects Loch Voil, in the north, to Lochs Vennacher and Callander in the south.

Below, stone cottages under a giant Douglas fir near Callander.

The Braes of Balquhidder run westwards from the Kingshouse Inn which lies on the main road through Strathyre, the valley which provides the main line of communication running north and south in western Perthshire, and links Stirling to Loch Tay and Loch Earn by way of Callander. As well as carrying the road the valley provided a passage for the now-derelict Callander and Oban Railway.

A little to the south of the Kingshouse Inn, the village of Strathyre straggles along the road, a collection of Victorian houses and eighteenth-century cottages. The village has an interesting tree-nursery providing for the afforestation schemes. Nearby is the birthplace of the Gaelic poet, Dugald Buchanan, who became schoolmaster at Rannoch and is commemorated by a memorial there.

Beyond Strathyre the road follows the attractive shore of Loch Lubnaig, "the bent loch." Across its waters Ben Ledi rises steeply and impressively, mirrored in the loch on the calm days which are frequent in this sheltered spot; but the placid, reed-fringed waters of the River Leny at its outflow from the loch belie the tumult to come when it plunges down the Falls of Leny on either side of a tooth of rock, and runs in rapids through a steep-sided gorge towards the foot of the valley. There road and railway jostle the stony river through the Pass of Leny, until it breaks out to join the Teith above Callander.

Here a main road westwards to the Trossachs follows the northern shore of Loch Vennacher under the shoulder of Ben Ledi, and close to the junction of the roads is Kilmahog, with an old toll-house, a small woollen mill with its own shop and a factory manufacturing fishing rods.

Callander.

Callander is a tourist centre, which has gained an additional interest for many from the fact that many parts of it can be identified with Tannoch Brae, the town in which A. J. Cronin's two doctors, Dr. Finlay and Dr. Cameron practised. The identification is not Cronin's: Callander was used in the television version of the stories.

The town is an eighteenth-century creation; built by the Commissioners for the forfeited estates on the Drummond lands after the Jacobite risings. At first it was a minor meeting point of roads, its natural strategic position having been recognised even by the Romans, for there is a camp there. The nineteenth century brought the railway and the twentieth the motor-car to make it a busy, thriving town. Its broad main street is lined with tweed and woollen shops, hotels and restaurants. Behind it substantial and attractive Victorian stone villas climb the foothills of Ben Each and beyond them is a pleasant walk up to the Bracklinn Falls. To the west, and dominating the views from the town, is Ben Ledi.

Close by Callander the Keltie joins the Teith, which runs down to feed the Forth just above Stirling. The road follows the river as far as the little town of Doune. Doune boasts an ancient royal castle and historic nineteenth-century cotton mills. The castle, which was never completed, is extremely well-preserved. It was confiscated from the dukes of Albany by James I and then in 1528 returned to the original family whence it passed to the earls of Moray. The Scottish ballad which tells of the murder of the "Bonnie Earl o' Moray" describes his lady waiting vainly in the Castle Doune for his return.

The equestrian statue of Bruce set up on the field of Bannockburn in 1964 and the centre of annual celebrations. It was erected on the 650th anniversary of the battle.

Dunblane Cathedral, overlooking the Water of Allen. Although built mainly in the 13th century, parts of the square tower are Norman work. Margaret Drummond, James IV's mistress, is buried here with her two sisters, all of them being poisoned in 1502.

A close neighbour to Doune is the ancient cathedral city of Dunblane, mercifully by-passed by the main Perth to Stirling road, so that despite its position it retains a considerable quiet charm. The oldest parts of its cathedral date from the twelfth century though its greatest beauties are Gothic thirteenth-century work. The cathedral lay in a sad state of dilapidation for centuries after the Reformation but was restored for use as a place of worship in the late nineteenth century. The personal collection of books of Bishop Robert Leighton, who later became Archbishop of Glasgow, is preserved in the town.

Dunblane was the ecclesiastical centre of the district: the secular power lay in Stirling. With the exception of Edinburgh no Scottish town is so steeped in history. It lies at the strategic centre of Scotland, commanding the Forth at what was historically its lowest bridge and sitting astride the main lines of communication between the north of Scotland and Glasgow to the west, Edinburgh to the east.

Two of the greatest battles of Scottish history were fought in the immediate neighbourhood. In 1297 an English army marched north on Stirling to quell William Wallace. They arrived to find Wallace drawn up on the foothills of the Ochils, north of the river. The English army began to cross the old wooden bridge of that time. Wallace attacked when "as many of the enemy as he believed he could overcome" had crossed, and the English were totally routed. The other battle, Bannockburn, is still more famous. Here Bruce defeated Edward II. In recent times the battlefield has been laid out as a park and an equestrian statue of Bruce has been erected.

The town of Stirling is dominated by the castle, and in certain respects resembles the pattern of the old town of Edinburgh, being built on a volcanic neck and tail with the castle occupying the steep bluff of the neck and the town straggling down the tail.

The old town is of great interest and is being thoughtfully and tactfully restored. Argyll's Lodging, which is now a youth hostel, is a superb example of a seventeenth-century town house. Close by stands the remarkable and never completed Mar's Wark, an ambitious though crude essay in Renaissance style, intended as a town house for the Earl of Mar.

The Church of the Holy Rude stands high on the Castle Hill, a fine Gothic building, dating for the most part from the fifteenth and sixteenth centuries and bearing scars of shot from Monk's siege in 1651. Mary Queen of Scots was crowned in this church at the age of nine months, and later in 1567 the year-old James VI was also crowned here with John Knox preaching a sermon for the occasion. Close by the church is Cowane's Hospital, generally known as the Guildhall, a charitable foundation of the seventeenth-century with a statue of its founder, John Cowane, together with his chest, his Bible and old Scots weights and measures. The foundation still distributes funds as outdoor relief.

The rest of the upper part of the old town consists of humbler but graceful town houses and tenements which are being restored. The new town, to the south of the Dumbarton Road, is attractive in a different way— spacious, with fine trees and spring flowers, dignified houses and terraces.

A view of Stirling from the Wallace Monument, with the Forth meandering through its flat valley.

Church of the Holy Rude, Stirling, the scene of the coronation of Mary Queen of Scots in 1543, at the age of nine months.

Mary Queen of Scots (1542-87).

Stirling Castle. The ramparts can be walked and provide striking views over the surrounding country.

The focal point of Stirling is, of course, the Castle. It is first of all superbly situated, commanding wide and distant views of the Forth valley to east and to west, with the range of the Ochils stretching out eastwards and Ben Lomond in the distance to the west.

The castle itself has suffered from continuous military occupation. The regimental headquarters of the Argyll and Sutherland Highlanders, it has had to be adapted to the needs of the barracks, but it is now being gradually restored. The outworks date from the eighteenth century though the Gatehouse is fifteenth century as is the Prince's Tower. The most interesting building is the ornate Palace, constructed between 1496 and 1540, its exterior ornamented with figures of soldiers and grotesques.

Prominent in the landscape is another famous viewpoint, the Wallace Monument, an elaborate baronial-style tower, 220 feet high, erected on Abbey Craig, where Wallace marshalled his army before the Battle of Stirling Bridge. The interior contains various relics, including Wallace's great sword.

Close below the monument are the beautiful and finely-wooded grounds of Airthrey Castle which have become the site of Scotland's new post-war university, the University of Stirling.

Immediately to the south of Abbey Craig is the ruin of Cambuskenneth Abbey, a twelfth-century foundation by David I for the Austin canons. James III and Margaret of Denmark, his queen, were buried here, and it has been used as a meeting place for the Scottish parliament.

A statue of Robert Burns stands in the gardens between Stirling library and the Municipal Buildings.

From Causewayhead, at the foot of the Wallace Monument, Hillfoots Road runs along the Ochils to Milnathort. It is an attractive route. The Ochils are not a high range, their summit Ben Cleuch being a mere 2,363 feet, but they rise steeply and impressively above the little hillfoot towns.

Most westerly of these is Alva, with thriving woollen, printing and jam-making industries. Behind the town is the famous Silver Glen, so called from its former mineral workings, but now a well-designed park in its lower part, with walks up the glen to a fine waterfall at its head.

Tillicoultry, a paper-making and woollens town, a few miles to the east, likewise has its glen path leading to the ascent of Ben Cleuch. The shoulder of the glen is somewhat disfigured by quarrying, but at least the quarry road gives easy access to fine views over the Forth valley.

The queen of the Hillfoots' towns is undoubtedly Dollar, a pleasant residential town given a somewhat academic atmosphere by the well-known Dollar Academy, a boarding and day school set in beautiful grounds and boasting a foundation building of considerable elegance designed by William Playfair, the well-known Edinburgh architect. Dollar Glen has paths which lead up a picturesque ravine, well-wooded and patterned with waterfalls, to Castle Campbell or Castle Gloom, a charming castle quite belying the latter name.

The road north to Perth at the eastern end of Hillfoots road follows Glenfarg, a narrow wooded pass through the eastern extremity of the Ochils in which river, road and railway jostle each other in the confined space, to burst out into eastern Strathearn and cross the River Earn on the way to Perth.

Right, Kirk of St. John the Baptist, Perth, where Charles I, Charles II and Bonnie Prince Charlie attended services.

Below, South Inch, Perth. A riddle claims that Perth is the smallest city in Scotland because it lies 'within two Inches'.

Perth, "the Fair City", commands the Tay at what was historically its lowest bridge just as Stirling commands the Forth. Like Stirling it is an historic city, but it has preserved few historical monuments. The greatest of these is the Kirk of St. John the Baptist, a noble fifteenth-century burgh church, with a fine spire and a magnificent collection of church pewter and silver ware.

For many centuries Perth was a centre of national government. Scottish kings were crowned at nearby Scone, and royal courts were often held at Perth. From the twelfth to the fifteenth centuries many Scottish parliaments were held in the town, and Church councils also met there. This former national prominence is reflected in the fact that the Lord Provost of Perth is second in precedence to the Lord Provost of Edinburgh.

The Salutation Hotel in South Street is said to be the oldest hotel in Scotland, and Bonnie Prince Charlie lodged there in 1745. It was from Perth that he proclaimed his father king. This was just one incident in the eventful and violent history of the city, which saw the Battle of the Clans on the North Inch in 1396, the assassination of James I in the Blackfriars Monastery in 1437, and the Gowrie Conspiracy of 1600.

Today Perth is a prosperous place with diversified industry including whisky distilleries, a large insurance company, dyeing and cleaning, jute and twine manufacturing, brewing, glass-making and printing and publishing. There are also important livestock markets including the famous bull sales held each February.

Perth also has a small but active port on the river, as befits a city whose river and the riverside Inches are its glory.

The River Tay at Kinnoull. The hunting tower perched on the cliff is a nineteenth-century folly, built to enhance the view.

From Perth the Tay broadens rapidly into a noble estuary. The southern bank has been isolated by the fact that it lies neither on road nor railway routes. Newburgh remains small and quiet, its prominence as a river port eclipsed, and between it and Wormit is a stretch of unspoiled countryside with villages which have a Highland primitiveness.

The north side of the river has a belt of fertile land, the Carse of Gowrie, backed by the southern spurs of the Sidlaw Hills, those near Perth being craggy and tree-covered, those nearer Dundee well-farmed. The Carse road is an attractive one. To the south is the broadening river, gay with sailing dinghies; to the north the hills rise steeply. Around stretches the rich red soil of the Carse, one of Scotland's premier soft-fruit growing areas.

Dundee, though an interesting city, is scarcely a beautiful one; but its siting is incomparable. Built on hills on the north bank of the Tay, it looks across the broad estuary to the fields and hills of Fife. Large houses testify to the traditional wealth of Dundee merchants, much of it founded on the connection with India which grew from the jute trade.

Dundee's hinterland is also attractive, mixing hills and glens with comfortably rich farming land. For the Dundee family returning from a day in the country, the view from the Black Watch memorial at the head of Powrie Brae, taking in the river, and the volcanic Dundee Law floating above the reek of the town, is a warming prospect, prelude to jam and scones at the fireside.

The Black Watch memorial looks out across Dundee and the mouth of the Tay.

L

Approaches to the Tay Road Bridge, Dundee, with the Firth of Tay looking out to the North Sea.

Dundee is traditionally famous for jute, jam and journalism, but its industry is much more broadly based than this and it is ranked by many as second industrially to Glasgow though by population it is Scotland's fourth city.

In the past Dundee was famous for coarse flax weaving and as a whaling centre. The two came together in the nineteenth century when jute fibre began to be imported from India. Whale oil made it workable and the flax-weavers' skill was turned to jute, an industry which still survives today as Dundee's staple. Jam and marmalade-making, food-canning and confectionary are important. There is a well-established shipbuilding tradition. New manufactures such as cash registers, watches, refrigerators and plastics have been developed. Also Dundee remains a centre of magazine publishing and of picture postcard and calendar printing.

The centre of Dundee, a cramped mass of tenements and jute mills which contrasted with the prosperous suburbs, was a product of the jute boom in the nineteenth century, and it deteriorated badly during the twentieth. The city is now the subject of a far-reaching scheme of urban renewal, and new shops and hotels are being erected in a unified city centre which is reminiscent of those in the new towns and regrettably lacking in character. However, it may be that time will bring mellowness.

Dundee has a tradition of extremely sound and effective education. The fame of her state schools, particularly the Morgan and Harris Academies, is reinforced by that of the independent Dundee High School. Recently, Queen's College, Dundee, formerly a constituent college of the University of St. Andrews, attained full and independent university status. Both the college of art and the technical college are expanding.

Dundee has now supplanted the historical position of Perth as the site of the lowest bridges on the Tay. The first to come were the railway bridges and the first of these, designed by Sir Thomas Bouch, was blown down with the loss of a passenger train in a gale on 28th December 1879. The piers of the old bridge can still be seen alongside the later bridge, which was built between 1883 and 1888 and is two miles long. The modern road bridge, which finally replaced the ferries and supplied ready access for cars to Fife, was completed in 1966.

On the Fife bank of the river, Newport, which was formerly the ferry station, developed during the nineteenth century as a residential suburb of Dundee. Tayport, which looks across the river to Broughty Ferry, was the station for an earlier ferry which declined after the Newport ferry and the railway bridge were opened. It is now a small town with a surprisingly active little harbour.

Beyond Tayport is the great flat sandy expanse of Tent's Muir, stretching up to the mouth of the Eden. Here the sea is receding extremely rapidly leaving an extensive area of sand which is being afforested and has a hundred-acre nature reserve rich in bird life.

Newport-on-Tay, founded in 1822 by Act of Parliament as the ferry station between Fife and Dundee.

At the southern end of Tent's Muir beside the River Eden is a major military airport at Leuchars, a village which is notable for the very fine early Romanesque church. The road crosses the Eden at Guard Bridge, a village built round a paper mill, and then strikes eastwards to St. Andrews, with the rolling links to the left of the road and the distinctive spires of the university city ahead.

Leuchars Church. The double arcades are authentic Norman work, probably executed 1183-7. The rest of the church is modern.

St. Andrews is a haunting—and haunted—old town with different moods in summer and in winter.

In summer it is a holiday resort. The long expanse of the West Sands is gay with children and bathers, the Castle and Cathedral thronged with tourists.

Golf is at its height and St. Andrews is a Mecca for the golfers of the world. The Royal and Ancient Golf Club, the premier in Britain, was founded in 1754, and the links were then already established. There are four eighteen-hole courses, the Old, the New, the Eden and the Jubilee. The Old Course remains one of the greatest courses in the world, largely because of its slow refinement out of a natural links setting. Consequently, St. Andrews acts as host to major tournaments.

Craigtoun Park, St. Andrews, its quaint buildings and bridges surrounded by flowers.

Outside the short summer season St. Andrews is a town dominated by its university, and when filled with students it has the air of being haunted by history. They bring to it enough life to recall its past glories without swamping it in the present.

The university is Scotland's oldest, dating from the foundation of St. Mary's College in 1410 by Bishop Laidlaw. St. Salvator's College and St. Leonard's College were added, the first founded by the beloved Bishop Kennedy, but, in the financial decline of the university in the eighteenth century, they were combined to form United College. The scarlet gown of St. Andrews is worn by students of United College, while students of St. Mary's, who are either theologians or post-graduates, wear a black gown.

St. Andrews students gathered in front of the quadrangle of St. Salvator's College.

The town itself has been safeguarded from contact with much of its modern suburban and estate development by its restricted site, with the sea to the north and east and the Kinness Burn to the south. The straggle of houses out the west road and the estates across the Burn are outside its spiritual walls. The true town is strung on three main streets running roughly east and west and converging towards the cathedral. Each has its own character.

North Street is broad and clean and bare and east-coast. It is dominated by the tower of the university chapel which forms one side of the main quadrangle of United College. The Younger Graduation Hall is an unpleasing error of taste, but the east end of the street compensates with some pleasant houses.

Market Street, the centre of the three, is close and crowded. It focusses on the cobbled market square with its two hotels, the west end of the street being a jumble of busy

The ruins of St. Andrews castle, formerly a Cardinal's palace, jutting over a rock formation known as 'the Scores'. From a window in the central tower Cardinal Beaton is said to have watched the burning of the Reformist martyr George Wishart.

shops and the east end a narrow lane.

South Street is a noble and elegant street. At the west end the arch of the old town gate opens into a broad thoroughfare softened by trees. Madras College, the burgh school, is set back from the road with the rudimentary ruin of Blackfriars Chapel in its forecourt. The town church of Holy Trinity is midway along South Street on its northern side and a little eastwards is the attractive courtyard containing St. Mary's College and the University Library. Eastwards from this stretches a row of historic town houses fit for the persons of position who once lived in the ecclesiastical and academic capital of Scotland.

The cathedral was once the largest church in Scotland and is even now impressive as a ruin. Built between the twelfth and fourteenth centuries, it was destroyed in the later sixteenth century when the iconoclastic assault of the reformers was followed by the depredations of the citizens of St. Andrews who used the cathedral as a convenient quarry for ready-dressed building stone. All that remains standing are considerable parts of both east and west gables and the south wall of the nave. Close by the east end is the remarkable St. Rule's tower, 108 feet in height and part of a disproportionately small twelfth-century church of the Augustinian canons, which the tower may in fact pre-date.

From the top of St. Rule's tower you can look westwards over the town to the west sands and the Eden mouth beyond the Castle or eastwards across the east sands to the Kinkell Braes and the Maiden Rock. Below lies the ancient harbour with its crooked pier along which the students traditionally walk in their red gowns after the Sunday morning chapel service. Above the harbour just outside the wall of the cathedral precinct is the site, now marked only by foundations, of the ancient Church of St. Mary of the Rock.

The other great ruin of St. Andrews is the Castle, which was the fortified episcopal palace. It is remarkable for its brutal bottle dungeon, carved in solid rock, and for a mine and countermine remaining from a siege. These are relics of a most turbulent past, which included the burning of the Protestant martyr, George Wishart, before the gates and the subsequent murder of the Cardinal Archbishop Beaton,

Crail Harbour.

The southward roads from St. Andrews lead to a string of villages of pleasant names sited along the coast between the most easterly point of the county, Fife Ness and Largo Bay: Crail, Anstruther, Pittenweem, St. Monance and Elie.

These are villages of a family, each individual yet each sharing common characteristics. Collectively they are often known as the Scottish Riviera, though an analogy with Brittany or Cornwall might be more accurate. All have a close communion with the sea, the lines of streets running down to the harbour, which is the natural centre of interest, and all now combine fishing and pleasure sailing with popularity as holiday resorts.

Crail is probably of all these the most picturesque and is much frequented by artists. Houses of different stones, grey and pink and red, jostle down the streets to the harbour in an artful irregularity which juxtaposes fronts and gables. At the top of the town the Marketgate has a more regular unity and contains many pleasant old houses, some of them going back to the seventeenth century.

Anstruther is larger and busier than Crail with a longer water front, crowded with shops to serve the visitors, but retaining much of its charm. Pittenweem has an ancient harbour from which the houses of the town are built up in steps as if audience to the business of the boats. St. Monance has a double harbour and boatbuilding yards and a most attractive fishermen's church abutting on the sea so that the wall of the graveyard is part of the sea wall. Elie is unusual in the grandeur of some of its houses for it was formerly a place of some commercial importance.

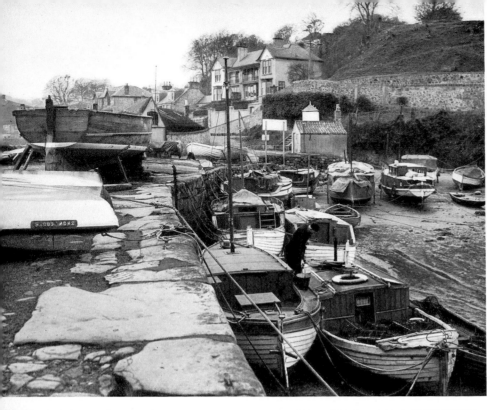

The harbour at Aberdour, on the Firth of Forth. Boat trips out to Inchcolm can be made from here.

Although there are other resorts to the west, Leven and Largo and the delightful Aberdour, yet the general character of this district of south Fife is of an industrial and mining area. The foundation of this development was historically the South Fife coalfield, but this is rapidly being run down, and the pit towns such as Kelty, Lochgelly and Valleyfield are feeling the contraction of the industry acutely.

The path to recovery would appear to be charted by the new town of Glenrothes, but it is a difficult way to follow for the old begrimed pit villages. Glenrothes was founded in 1949 to house the miners who would work a new coal seam from a radically modern pit. But the seam proved unworkable and instead Glenrothes has had to attract new industries on which to base its economy.

Outside the mining communities there are also some well established industries in this part of Fife—paper in Markinch; textiles, plastics and papermills in Leslie; shipbuilding in Burntisland; and paper-making and ship-breaking in Inverkeithing.

The industrial capital of the area, Kirkcaldy, was a linoleum town, the industry having been started by Michael Nairn in 1847; and linoleum and floor-coverings are still important products, though supplemented by such industries as engineering, rope-spinning and linen-weaving.

Kirkcaldy is a town with a marked character which is not easy to define. Partly this is associated with its nickname "the Lang Toun". Its main street is nearly four miles long, and it gives a sense of district more familiar in a larger city. Partly, too, the character of Kirkcaldy derives from the strength and humour of its people: it mixes seafolk and factory-folk.

The Protestant Church at Glenrothes. At the far end is a mural depicting scenes from the life of Christ, painted by Albert Morrocco.

Inland from the industrial area is a district of pleasing country and small country towns, focussed on the distinctive Lomond Hills and Loch Leven. The Lomond Hills are a low range culminating at either end in the twin peaks of East Lomond (1,471 feet) and West Lomond (1,713 feet), which gain in character from their isolation in comparatively flat country.

The small royal burgh of Falkland, the birthplace of Richard Cameron, the Covenanter, lies under the East Lomond. Its glory is the palace, built by the Stuart kings as a hunting lodge, and frequented and embellished by James III, James IV and James V, the last of whom reputedly died here in the King's Room, shortly after the birth of his daughter, Mary Queen of Scots. It was on hearing the news of her birth that he is said to have pronounced his celebrated doom on the Stuart monarchy: "It cam' wi' a lass and it will gang wi' a lass." The beautiful palace with its Catholic chapel is the home of Major Michael Crichton Stuart, its hereditary Constable, though it is in the charge of the National Trust for Scotland.

Across the hills lies Loch Leven, with its island castle in which Mary Queen of Scots was imprisoned in 1567-8, only to escape and make westwards to the debacle of the Battle of Langside. The loch is now noted for its angling, and as a sanctuary for water-fowl.

A view of Falkland, showing (l. to r.) the Palace, the Town House (1805) and the Church, built by O. Tyndall-Bruce in the mid-nineteenth century. In the background is the gentle slope of the Lomond Hills.

Kinross House, a beautiful seventeenth-century manor whose gardens have won international fame.

Kinross, the county town of the small county of Kinross-shire, lies close by the loch, separated from it by the grounds of Kinross House, an elegant seventeenth-century mansion built by Sir William Bruce. The fame of the loch has made the town an angling centre.

In the little town the elements of Low Country and Dutch architectural influence anointed with Kinross-shire and Fife are still clearly seen, elements which distinguish these neat buildings with their crow-stepped gables and pantiled roofs from the rest of rural Scotland. The kirks, with their bulky towers and low squat steeples perched above, are quite particular to this neighbourhood and indicative of its independent development. In addition the area is noted for rich farmland.

The Forth Estuary from Alloa downwards is not merely impressive, but also an economically important waterway. That it has been so for centuries is testified to by the remarkable survival of the fascinating little royal burgh of Culross.

In the sixteenth and seventeenth centuries Culross traded in salt and coal and was a port for northern Europe. When its trade declined, progress passed it by, and it has consequently been preserved, an almost intact example of a small Scots town of the past. Above the town is an abbey from which a steep causeway leads down to the lower town with its Mercat Cross surrounded by old houses, many of them on a scale that speaks of past prosperity. Most remarkable of all is the beautifully preserved "Culross Palace".

Culross, the Mercat Cross in the centre of this strikingly beautiful old village.

A fine example of Scottish Baronial style in Inverkeithing.

Almost due south from Kinross, the historic town of Dunfermline commands the approach to the River Forth. Dunfermline was formerly a royal seat, and its abbey was founded by Queen Margaret, the wife of Malcolm Canmore, after whom the Queensferry across the River Forth was named. The abbey has a noble and sturdy Norman nave of the mid-twelfth century and a fine Norman west doorway. King Robert the Bruce was buried here and his remains were identified when unearthed during the early nineteenth century by evidence of the removal of his heart from the body in accordance with his dying wishes.

Across the river, Grangemouth has become the busiest seaport on the east coast of Scotland, with double the annual cargo of Leith. Apart from the docks, Grangemouth is a boom-town of oil and plastics.

Leith is the historic premier port of the Forth and though recently overshadowed by Grangemouth it is still important. From the days of Robert the Bruce until the Reform Act of 1832 it came, as the port of Edinburgh, under the superiority of Edinburgh, and since 1920 it has been incorporated in the city. It was frequently the target of English raids and was twice sacked in the sixteenth century. Its considerable docks, which include dry dock and graving dock facilities, have recently been modernized, and the town is confident of its future. But it is also proud of its past. Care is being taken as the town is renewed to preserve the best of the past. The old dwelling known as Lamb's House, for example, has been well-restored and the public buildings such as the Assembly Rooms and the Corn Exchange will not be lost. Modernisation will leave Leith the traditional character of a long-established port.

Lamb's House in Water's Close, Leith. Originally a merchant's house, where Mary Queen of Scots was entertained after her landing in 1561, it has now been restored as an Old Folks' Home.

174

Dunfermline Abbey—a Benedictine house and the resting place of King Robert the Bruce.

But the Forth is not to be thought of merely as a commercial waterway. There are fascinating islands in the Firth, and many pleasant spots along its shores which are a far cry from the commercial traffic of Grangemouth and Leith.

Of the islands the most interesting are Inchcholm off Aberdour, and Inchkeith, which lies off Leith.

Inchcolm appeared on the stage of history when Alexander I, seeking shelter there during a stormy crossing of the river, was given such hospitality as was available by a resident Columban hermit. In gratitude he founded on the island the Abbey of St. Columba, an Augustinian house, and Inchcolm like Iona became a holy place. The remains of the abbey are still well preserved.

Inchkeith is famous for a legend worth repeating and a visit worth recording. The legend is that James IV, in order to conduct some research into the primitive speech of mankind, marooned on Inchkeith two infants whom he placed in the charge of a dumb women so that their speech should not be learned from their elders. Report has it that when recovered they spoke good Hebrew!

The visit was that of Dr. Johnson who "stalked like a giant among the luxuriant thistles and nettles" and was much taken with the potential of the island which, he thought, would quickly have been bought up and exploited had it lain in the same proximity to London as it did to Edinburgh. Boswell reports him as saying: "I'd have this island. I'd build a house, make a good landing-place, have a garden, and vines, and all sorts of trees. A rich man, of a hospitable turn, here, would have many visitors from Edinburgh."

Inchcolm Abbey, in the Firth of Forth. The original nave was Norman but was completely altered. The octagonal chapter house and the choir, however, date from the thirteenth century.

Cramond, former fishing village on the south side of the Firth of Forth, is now a haven for yachtsmen.

On the southern side of the Forth, Linlithgow and Cramond are both worthy of attention.

Linlithgow, the county town of West Lothian, lies inland from the river beside Linlithgow Loch. It is an historic town, one of David I's royal burghs, with an attractive centre of which the showpieces are the Palace and the Church of St. Michael. The Palace was probably founded by David I, though the oldest part of the present structure is the tower built by Edward I in 1302. It was a favourite Stuart palace and Mary Queen of Scots was born here in 1542.

Cramond, with easy access from Edinburgh by a good road is a charmingly restored village which serves the pleasure sailing needs of Edinburgh as Leith serves the city with commercial shipping.

For many people the fame of the Forth River itself is eclipsed by the fame of its bridges. The Queensferry Passage was a traditional ferry point, the river narrowing about here to a width of $1\frac{1}{4}$ miles, and it is across this relatively narrow, but deep stretch of the Forth that the two great bridges stride.

The railway bridge, with its famous cantilevered arches, was built between 1883 and 1890, an earlier design by Sir Thomas Bouch having been cancelled at the last minute after the failure of his Tay Bridge. The mass of the structure is impressive, but indicative of design techniques far more primitive than those employed in the slender single-span suspension road bridge which replaced the ferry in 1964. The towers are 512 feet high and the central span 3,300 feet.

The road bridge across the Firth of Forth is the second longest suspension bridge in Europe, fifth in the world.

M

The old and new Edinburgh seen from Salisbury Crags, to the south-east.

Below left, a painting by Sir David Wilkie of Knox preaching to The Lords of The Congregation, including the Earls of Morton and Argyll and the Countess of Argyll. This picture, a replica of one in the Tate Gallery, may be seen in the National Gallery of Scotland.

Below right, John Knox's House in the Royal Mile. Knox may have lived here 1561-2 whilst minister of St. Giles.

The great Forth bridges are the modern gateway from the north to the grey majesty of Edinburgh, more ancient as a city than as a capital. Its foundations lie in religious and military settlements, the castle which occupies the site of a very early fortified settlement and the Abbey of Holyrood, founded in 1128. Between the two the old Edinburgh grew, stretching down the slope from the castle ramparts to the Abbey, later a palace, that lay beneath Arthur's Seat. To the north it was hemmed in by the Nor' Loch and its eastern marshes. To the south it was consolidated for the sake of defence.

About 1450, James II adopted Edinburgh as his seat and began to hold his parliaments there so that, without any formal declaration, Edinburgh succeeded Perth as the capital of Scotland. In 1513 the Scottish army assembled before Flodden on the Borough Muir and after that tragic battle the Flodden Wall was hastily thrown up to defend the city from the south. Henry VIII, however, devastated Edinburgh in 1544 and again in 1547. The Union of the Crowns brought freedom from English invasion, but when James VI and I moved to London, his nobles and his court followed him, and Edinburgh became something of a hollow capital.

She remained, however, a centre of religious life and of religious disturbance. John Knox had been Minister of St. Giles from 1559 to 1572 and had established a tradition of radical presbyterianism. It was in his church in 1637 that Jeannie Geddes reputedly threw her stool at Dean Hannay when he was reading Laud's service book. And a year later at Greyfriars the National Covenant was signed.

The Old Town of Edinburgh has as its spine the Royal Mile, the long irregular line of streets, which leads down the ridge of the castle hill from the Castle at its summit to Holyrood Palace at its lower end. Until two hundred years ago this street, the Grassmarket and the streets off them were virtually the whole of the city. And trapped on its confined rock, Edinburgh built high. The mile is lined with great tenements or "lands", the skyscrapers of their day, in which people of wealth and fashion once lived.

Immediately below the esplanade of the castle is Castle Hill, a narrow street dominated by the Outlook Tower, which houses a camera obscura. From here a crooked way runs down to the Grassmarket below the Castle on the south, which was the scene of executions and public hangings in the past.

Below Castle Hill, the Mile broadens into the Lawnmarket, lined by tall old tenements including St. James's Court, where Dr. Johnson stayed as the guest of Boswell. Architecturally most interesting is Gladstone's Land, now preserved by the National Trust for Scotland and the Saltire Society.

The centre of the Royal Mile is the High Street, linking the Lawnmarket and the Canongate, which runs down to the palace; and at the centre of High Street life is the High Kirk of St. Giles—in spite of Presbyterian egalitarianism, undoubtedly the premier church in Scotland. Here too is the legal centre of Scotland, for behind St. Giles is Parliament Square and the Parliament House, now used for the supreme Scottish Courts of Justice and from 1639 until 1707 also the meeting place of the Scottish Parliament.

Holyrood Palace, the west facade built by Sir William Bruce in the 1670s for Charles II.

179

Holyrood Palace at the lower end of the Royal Mile is pictured here from the south with the town and the Firth of Forth behind it.

The Old Town is anchored in the past at both ends. At the bottom of the Royal Mile stands Holyrood Palace and at the top the Castle.

James IV built the first palace beside Holyrood Abbey founded by David I, but it was burnt by the English, in 1543, and again under the Commonwealth. The present building was executed largely under Charles II, and Charles Edward held the last Stuart levee here in 1745. It is now quite frequently used by the monarch and also houses the Lord High Commissioner during General Assemblies of the Church of Scotland.

The oldest building in the Castle—and in Edinburgh—is St. Margaret's Chapel, dating from 1076. The Castle itself, which contains the regalia of Scotland, is of all periods. It provides a dramatic skyline for the city.

It is the Castle and the skyline of the Old Town that dominate Princes Street, the busiest shopping street of the modern city. Princes Street is one of the best situated streets in the world, but its glory is in the view it commands rather than in itself. The conglomeration of shop-fronts would not distinguish it from the shopping street of any industrial city were it not that it is one-sided and looks across low-set gardens to the rock and the Old Town.

The gardens, Waverley Station and the railway occupy what was formerly the site of the Nor' Loch. In the late eighteenth century Lord Provost Drummond drained the Loch and threw North Bridge across the marshes at its eastern end. Subsequently, the railway came and the site was laid out with attractive gardens and monuments.

The floodlit castle stands dramatically on the skyline above Princes Street, challenged by the Gothic spire of the Scott monument.

181

Below, an engraving of St. George's Church, now converted into an extension of H.M. Register House, Scotland, for storing documents.

Bottom, looking east along George Street to the 150-foot Melville Monument in St. Andrew Square.

The New Town of Edinburgh is one of the great glories of the city. As Edinburgh grew, the gentry and prosperous professional people fretted at the crowded life of the Old Town tenements. The draining and bridging of the noisome Nor' Loch opened the splendid site offered by the hill on its north bank, which sloped away to the Firth of Forth. This opportunity was exploited with a splendid sense of style, dignity and elegance.

The New Town was built as a unity, begun on designs by James Craig and completed in detail by architects who worked for the most part harmoniously in the spirit of the first designs. George Street is the spine of the New Town as the Royal Mile is of the Old, but what a contrast in spirit! The Royal Mile is a tangle of uneven buildings, romantic, untidy and formerly insanitary: George Street is spacious and noble, ending in two squares, the elegant Charlotte Square at the West End, St. Andrew Square at the east only slightly marred by a pretentiousness which makes it somewhat out of scale. Princes Street is the outlier to the south, the one-sided Queen Street to the north. At the intersections of the cross streets are statues and sudden views across the Forth to the hills of Fife.

The New Town was built from 1770 onwards into the nineteenth century. The world of fashion and wealth and intellect soon shifted across the Nor' Loch, David Hume one of the first. Edinburgh became "the Athens of the North", her drawing rooms filled with eloquent and witty conversation, her Assembly Rooms with elegance and fashion. The New Town brought in Edinburgh's Golden Age.

It was an age of reason and intelligence and the drawing rooms of the New Town were the scene of parties where people met not to eat, but to talk and to listen. The *Edinburgh Review* and *Blackwood's Magazine* were in their heyday. The *Scotsman* was founded in 1817. Edinburgh talked about Hume's philosophy and Scott's novels, Gentlemen's Subscription Concerts and theatre.

Modern Edinburgh will never match that outburst of intelligence and curiosity, but her intellectual life is well-founded. There is the university, the youngest of the old four, founded in 1582, but quick to establish a world reputation, particularly for medicine. The "Old College" quadrangle is in the Old Town, though in the spirit of the New, for it was designed by Robert Adam and Playfair. Nowadays the buildings spread extensively, to house some 8,000 students.

Edinburgh is also rich in museums and libraries. The Royal Scottish Museum has strong collections of art, archaeology, ethnology and technology. There is also a unique and charming Museum of Childhood with a collection of toys and books, and the City Museum in the restored Huntly House in the Canongate. As well as a good municipal library, there is the National Library of Scotland, formerly the Advocate's Library, which has a collection third in importance to the British Museum and the Oxford Bodleian. The Scottish National Portrait Gallery and Museum of Antiquities in Queen Street is the premier collection for students of Scottish history, and there are important collections and exhibitions of art in the National Gallery and the Royal Scottish Academy at the foot of the Mound. Finally, for the biologist there are the Royal Botanic Gardens and the Royal Scottish Zoological Society's zoo.

Bellevue Crescent and St. Mary's Parish Church.

Edinburgh Castle.

Edinburgh is still a capital in this, that she is incomparably endowed to play the host to visitors to Scotland. Her natural setting with the towering castle and the backcloth of Arthur's Seat and the Salisbury Crags is arrestingly dramatic. The Old Town embodies all that is romantic; the New Town all that is classic. She is well equipped with hotels and restaurants, with shops and galleries. What is missing is the lively theatre and the plentiful music of London or Paris, but this Edinburgh provides at least for three weeks of each year in her International Festival of Music and Drama.

The Edinburgh Festival was started in 1947 on the initiative of the impresario, Rudolph Bing, who persuaded a group of Edinburgh citizens to back his idea. The Festival has been criticised a good deal as not being sufficiently Scottish, but it is in intention emphatically an international event, in which the city entertains performers as well as audiences.

There are concerts of orchestral and chamber music, opera, ballet and drama, with performers attracted from all over the world. One happy feature is that the specifically Scottish contributions, though limited, have been for the most part very successful. Allan Ramsay's pastoral ballad opera, *The Gentle Shepherd,* performed by candlelight, John Home's *Douglas* and *The Highland Fair* have been well-received, but the most astonishing and most overwhelming success has been reserved for a play in Middle Scots, *Ane Satire of the Thrie Estatis* by Sir David Lyndsay of the Mount. A recurrent success too is the searchlight military tattoo on the Castle Esplanade which takes advantage of the natural drama of the Castle and its setting.

In sharp contrast to the glamour of the capital, the country to the west of Edinburgh on the road to Glasgow is workaday and industrial. The busy Edinburgh to Glasgow road is not one generally recommended to the tourist unless he has a special interest in industrial history, but it leads to and through the working heart of Scotland.

Bathgate in West Lothian is in itself an essay in economic history. In the seventeenth century it was a weaving town, and later coal-mining was developed. In the mid-nineteenth century, Dr. James Young set up the first commercial paraffin refinery at nearby Whitburn, based on the oil shales of the area and this became a major enterprise at a time when paraffin lamps were the commonest form of domestic lighting. Now since the Second World War, a large factory for the manufacture of commercial vehicles

and tractors has been built along the main road, and Bathgate has stepped into the twentieth century with a vengeance.

Kirk o' Shotts, a village on the dreary moors half way between Edinburgh and Glasgow, though it dates from the fifteenth century at least, is also known for a symbol of the twentieth century, the 750 foot television mast, which handles transmissions for the midland belt of Scotland including both Glasgow and Edinburgh. But a television mast does not bring employment and the dour village remains a depressed area.

Beyond Kirk o' Shotts the road descends and branches lead off to the major towns of the Scottish "black country": Coatbridge and Motherwell, the great iron and steel towns whose flaring blast furnaces light the night sky, and their attendant industrial neighbours, Airdrie and Wishaw.

Bathgate, showing the open-cast mining which is now minimal. At one time silver was mined here, and shale-oil deposits provided paraffin for use as an early antiseptic in Edinburgh hospitals.

The coast and country to the east of Edinburgh contrasts strongly with the industrial complex to the west. East Lothian is predominantly an agricultural county, with rich arable farming in the northern plain and sheep-walks on the Lammermuir Hills along the southern boundary.

Haddington, the county town, is graced by Adam buildings, which have been beautifully maintained by the royal burgh, energetic and prosperous in the present but proud and careful of its past. Haddington's history was turbulent and dangerous, for the town lay on the route of English armies marching north on Edinburgh, and was several times sacked and burned. At the Knox Memorial Institute, the successor of the burgh school, both the poet William Dunbar and John Knox were educated, and Jane Welsh Carlyle and Samuel Smiles, the author of *Self Help*, were born in the town.

Aberlady, the former port for Haddington, has now declined into a residential village for Edinburgh commuters attracted by the pleasant East Lothian coast, which, apart from its beaches and harbours, is one of the great golfing centres of Scotland.

Prestonpans in the west was founded on saltpans, sharing with its neighbour, Cockenzie, a salt industry which, until the nineteenth century supplied the whole of the East of Scotland. The Battle of Prestonpans, at which the Jacobite army of Prince Charles Edward routed in ten minutes the English force of Sir John Cope was a high point of Jacobite hopes in the '45. Cockenzie, as well as sharing the salt industry, was an important fishing port.

Haddington, the alleged birthplace of John Knox. The south wall of the church bears bullet marks resulting from a clash between the English and a combined Scottish and French force in 1548.

Tantallon Castle, built in the characteristic red stone of the Lothian coast, is a grim relic of fiercer days.

Gullane is a golfing centre with three full eighteen-hole courses. Nearby North Berwick, whose sandy bays and attractive harbour make it the premier holiday resort on this stretch of coast, also has two fine golf courses.

Not far east of North Berwick the substantial ruin of Tantallon Castle, built in the rose-red local stone, stands out superbly on the cliffs. There is a massive frontal curtain wall flanked by round towers, which must have daunted the besiegers in days gone by when the castle was the impregnable stronghold of the Douglases.

The man-made fortress looks out over one made by nature, the steep-sided Bass Rock, which was successfully held from 1691 to 1694 after the Battle of Killiecrankie by a group of Jacobite officers.

Just to the east of the large bay at the outlet of the River Tyne, is the town of Dunbar, an ancient royal burgh and seaport, which, like so many others, has now become mainly a holiday and golfing resort. The church with its tall tower and lofty site is a fisherman's landmark, and above the harbour are the shattered ruins of the ancient castle, associated with "Black Agnes", the Countess of March and Dunbar who in 1339 successfully defended the castle under a six weeks' siege by the Earl of Salisbury. She is said to have shown her contempt for his efforts by dusting the battlements with her lace handkerchief in the face of his army. Mary Queen of Scots stayed in Dunbar Castle with Darnley after the murder of Rizzio, and later with Bothwell after the murder of Darnley.

The swimming pool at Dunbar, an ancient town whose history is gaily ignored by Scottish children every summer.

Immediately to the south of East Lothian lies the border county of Berwickshire, anomalous in taking its name from a town which though disputed between the Scots and the English for many centuries, finally became English, having been ceded in 1482. For some time after that it was an independent town serving as a bastion against the Scots, but it is now incorporated in Northumberland. Nevertheless, it remains at least part Scots, if on no stronger grounds than that its football team plays in the Scottish, not the English, League. It is now the doorstep of Scotland, outside the house but commanding the entrance with its bridges, the Old Bridge and its modern supplement carrying the roads and the famous Royal Border Bridge carrying the railway.

Greenlaw was the county town of Berwickshire from 1696 until 1853, when the honour passed to Duns, where it has remained. Duns was originally built on Duns Law, an ancient dun or hill fort, but the old town was destroyed by the English in 1548 and the present town beneath the Law was built in 1588. On the summit of the Law there now stands a stone commemorating the encampment in 1639 of the Covenanting Army commanded by Alexander Leslie and the Earl of Rothes. Duns other claim to fame is disputed with rivals; but the town is the most likely of all claimants to be the birthplace in 1266 of the famous medieval theologian Duns Scotus. The area seems to have been prolific of thinkers for a few miles to the east, close by the T-shaped village of Chirnside, is Ninewells, where the most famous of modern Scottish philosophers, David Hume, was born.

The southern boundary of Berwickshire follows the Tweed until the last couple of miles where England bites in to encompass Berwick.

The most important place on this stretch of the river is Coldstream, built on the site of an old ford near the junction of the Leet and the Tweed, which has been supplanted in modern times by a fine bridge constructed by John Smeaton in 1766. "Crossing the Tweed" is synonomous with going to Scotland and not surprisingly Coldstream, like Gretna Green in the west, has its "Old Marriage House" where runaway couples from the south came to enjoy the advantages of Scots Law. On the north side of the square is the original headquarters of the Coldstream Guards, the regiment which marched to London in 1660 and secured the restoration of Charles II.

The Hirsel, the famous seat of the Earls of Home, lies close to Coldstream and contains woods famous for their birds as well as a lake which is a wildfowl sanctuary. Berwickshire is distinguished for its fine castles and country houses. Hume Castle, another and more ancient seat of the Home family, is close to Greenlaw, as is the splendid classical mansion, Marchmont House, completed in the mid-eighteenth century for George Baillie by John and Robert Adam.

Another splendid Berwickshire castle is Thirlstane which stands on the Leader Water close to the royal burgh of Lauder. Thirlstane was originally built in the late sixteenth century for Maitland of Thirlstane, but it was extended and sumptuously decorated just after the Restoration in the high style of that period.

Thirlestane Castle, built in 1590 but greatly extended. The interior is decorated in particularly splendid Restoration style and houses collections of china, furniture and paintings.

Eyemouth, a fishing town of narrow alleys that formerly fostered many smugglers, their contraband goods being hidden in the cliff caves.

The Berwickshire coast is rocky and runs to sensational cliffs. The most striking natural feature is St. Abb's head, a rocky promontory riddled with smugglers' caves and capped by a lighthouse. Just to the north are the fragmentary ruins of Fast Castle, historically the stronghold of Logan of Restalrig, but more famous from its acceptance as the prototype of "Wolf's Crag" in Scott's *Bride of Lammermoor,* where Caleb Balderstone ran the penurious household of the Master of Ravenswood.

To the south of St. Abb's head the rough and generally inhospitable coast gives lodgement to the two pleasant fishing villages of St. Abb's and Burnmouth and to the busy fishing town of Eyemouth with a Smeaton harbour and pleasant beaches.

At the western extremity of Berwickshire on the border with Roxburghshire, fairyland and Christianity meet.

Near the town of Earlston is the ruin of the Rhymer's Tower, which is held to be the home of Sir Thomas Learmount, the thirteenth-century Scottish poet and seer, also known as Thomas the Rhymer and True Thomas, whose powers were attributed to a seven-year sojourn with the Queen of the Fairies.

A little to the south is one of the great border abbeys, Dryburgh, which was founded in 1150 by Hugh de Morville and colonised by monks from Alnwick. The closeness of the English border made Dryburgh vulnerable and it was destroyed three times in the fourteenth century. The abbey church is a ruin, but the cloister is well-preserved.

Dryburgh Abbey, a victim of border raids, contains the tombs of Earl Haig and Sir Walter Scott.

The inland county of Peeblesshire is often called Tweeddale after the great river which rises in the county and flows for almost half its course within its borders. The Tweed is a great anglers' river for both salmon and trout and has yielded the largest salmon ever caught in Scotland, a fish of 69¾ lbs. taken by the Earl of Home in 1730. But the Tweed and the country around it has captured the imagination of many who are not fishermen.

The county town, Peebles, is a prosperous royal burgh serving as a social focus for the pastoral farming area around it and as a tourist centre. It also has a thriving woollen industry, established over hundreds of years and manufacturing both woven tweeds and knitwear, which are renowned for their excellence throughout the world. The "Riding of the Marches", in fact an old Beltane Festival, which used to be held on 1st of May but is now in late June, has always attracted visitors, including James I.

Just west of the town and standing above the River Tweed, is Neidpath Castle, incomparably romantic in its setting. In its origins it was a Fraser stronghold, but it passed to the Hays of Tweeddale and then in 1686 was bought by the 1st Duke of Queensberry. It now belongs to the Earl of Wemyss.

Innerleithen, lower down the Tweed than Peebles, is a spa whose nineteenth-century popularity was sealed by Scott's novel, *St. Ronan's Well*, and since that time the name has been adopted for the spring, which was originally known as Doo's Well. Innerleithen has a border woollen industry as well as its tourist trade and the annual Border Games.

Below, Jedburgh Abbey, built in the late twelfth century and in ruins since 1523 when it was besieged by an English force under the Earl of Surrey.

Bottom, Hawick, with the baronial tower of the Town Hall dominating the High Street. The 'Common Riding' is a popular event here every June.

Of all the border counties, perhaps Roxburghshire is most representative of border tradition in its scenery, its towns, its towers and its abbeys. The heart of the county is the River Teviot and Teviotdale.

The village of Roxburgh is a small, quiet place and the county town is Jedburgh which stands on a tributary of the Teviot, the Jed Water, and commands the road into Scotland from Newcastle over Carter Bar. It is an ancient town, whose church was mentioned in the ninth century, but its antiquity is reflected in its plan round the market square rather than in its buildings, for it was completely destroyed by the English in the sixteenth century. Jedburgh Castle, which had often been occupied by the English, was dismantled in 1409 because it appeared to serve the English invader better than the Scots defender.

Jedburgh has a large rayon factory, but the industrial capital of the area and its largest town is Hawick, the most famous knitwear centre in Scotland, a town reputedly dominated by women owing to the preponderance of female labour in the knitting industry. But Hawick is famous for manly pursuits as well. Its rugby team is one of the best and toughest in Scotland and the Chase in its Common Riding is hair-raising.

The southern part of the county rises to the Cheviot Hills and the border land with England. To the north of the Teviot basin and overlooking the Tweed are the triple peaks of the Eildon Hills, reputedly split into three by Michael Scot, the Border Wizard, in an attempt to satisfy the appetite for work of a demon whom he was bound to keep occupied.

The Mill Lade at Melrose in the Spring.

Melrose, the little town which figures as "Kennaquhair" in Scott's *Monastery* and *Abbot*, lies beneath the Eildon Hills on the bank of the Tweed. Its glory is the ruined abbey, a Cistercian house founded by David I in 1136 and colonized from Rievaulx in Yorkshire. Melrose abbey suffered terribly from its proximity to the English border, being badly damaged by Edward II in 1322, utterly destroyed by Richard II in 1385 and laid waste once more in 1545. It never fully recovered from this attack.

Most of the standing parts which now remain date from the late fourteenth to the sixteenth centuries and they include much elaborate carving and tracery. A stone tablet commemorates John Morow or Moreau, a master mason who worked on the church.

196

Kelso lies at the junction of the Teviot and the Tweed. It too has a famous abbey, one of the strong and simple Tironensian foundations. Kelso abbey was first founded at Selkirk about 1113 by David I, while he was still Earl of Huntingdon, and was removed to Kelso in 1128 during his kingship. Little remains of the cloister, but the ruin of the church shows it to be the most spectacular expression of Romanesque architecture in Scotland.

The third of the great Roxburghshire abbeys is the Augustinian house at Jedburgh, also founded by David I, about 1138. Like the other border abbeys, Jedburgh suffered at the hands of the English, but the choir and tower and complete but roofless nave of remarkable and unusual design make Jedburgh an impressive monument to piety.

Kelso, described by Scott as "the most beautiful if not the most romantic village in Scotland".

197

Left, Sir Walter Scott as painted by James Hall in 1828.

Below, Abbotsford House on the south bank of the Tweed. The rooms have remained unchanged since Scott's lifetime and his collection of books and relics is on public show.

Yetholm, a few miles south-east of Kelso, is a double village comprising Town Yetholm and Kirk Yetholm. Historically its main claim to fame is as the headquarters of the Scottish gypsies and of their "royal family" the Faas. The last gypsy queen, Esther Faa Blythe, died in 1883 and the dynasty is now extinct. But it has been well-commemorated by Sir Walter Scott in the character of Meg Merrilies, drawn from Jean Gordon, the wife of Patrick Faa.

Scott himself is generally most closely associated with the county of Roxburghshire, and his famous house, Abbotsford, is close to Melrose. The famous author was born in Edinburgh in 1771, the son of a border couple, his father a Writer to the Signet. In his third year he was sent to his grandfather's farm of Sandyknowe near Smailholm where he learnt the old border stories and ballads as part of his growing up. At eight he went to Edinburgh High School and later to Edinburgh University before training as an advocate.

The Lay of the Last Minstrel, which he published in 1805, made him the most popular author of the day. *Waverley* was published anonymously in 1814 and was wildly successful. There followed the immense production of the Waverley novels.

Scott bought the Roxburghshire farm of Clarty Hole in 1811 and erected his ambitious baronial house there between 1816 and 1823. Financial disaster hit him in 1826 and the years until his death in 1832 were a time of desperate overwork as he wrote to clear his debts. Abbotsford was preserved for his successors by a subscription of his friends. A generous soul, he was, as he deserved to be, greatly loved.

Right, St. Mary's Loch, three miles by half a mile, with Tibbie Shiel's Inn on the neck of the isthmus which separates this loch from the Loch of the Lowes.

Below, Ettrick Water with Selkirk on its banks.

The county of Selkirk or Ettrick Forest, flanked by Roxburgh, Peebles and Dumfries, is the geographical heart of the Scottish borders. It was once a royal hunting ground, but is now a quiet, pastoral county, watered by the Ettrick and the Yarrow which flows out of St. Mary's Loch. Between St. Mary's Loch and the smaller Loch of the Lowes stands Tibbie Shiel's Inn, formerly an angler's hostelry kept by Isabella Richardson (Tibbie Shiel) and site of one of the famous Blackwood's Magazine "Noctes Ambrosianae" of Christopher North and James Hogg. Close by is a statue of James Hogg, "the Ettrick Shepherd", who was discovered as a poet by Scott and made his reputation with *The Queen's Wake*. The most famous of his poems, *Kilmeny*, is still read and loved. The whole area of Ettrick and Yarrow is rich in poetical associations, among the most famous, Wordsworth's praises of Yarrow.

The county town, Selkirk, stands on a hill overlooking the Ettrick Water. In days gone by it was a storm centre of the Anglo-Scottish raids and wars, and was burnt by the English in 1513 after Flodden. In the Selkirk Common Riding the standard-bearer is said to represent the town's sole survivor of that disastrous battle.

The town has an association with Sir Walter Scott, who was sheriff of the county, and with the African explorer, Mungo Park, who was born nearby at Foulshiels. Both are commemorated by statues.

Selkirk, now a woollen town like its border neighbours, was once famous as the centre of the Scottish shoemaking industry, and its inhabitants are still sometimes nicknamed "the souters (shoemakers) of Selkirk."

The great border town of Peebles has a magnificent setting in the Tweed valley. In the foreground is historic Neidpath Castle.

The Borders—Dumfries, Berwick, Ettrick and Teviotdale—are historically the bulwark of Scotland, glowering across the old Roman Wall at Cumberland and Northumberland, ancient enemies, rich in cattle. Much of the border minstrelsy is concerned with valour or treachery in the wars and forays against the English. To-day the enmity has abated, but in terms of language, loyalties and habits the frontier is still surprisingly sharply drawn. Carlisle is certainly English: Dumfries is unmistakably Scots.

The other aspect of the Borders is inward-looking, turning north towards the heartland of Scotland. The Clyde rises a few miles north-west of Moffat to flow through the orchards of Lanarkshire to the Scottish black-country and the great mart of Glasgow. And Glasgow herself sits at the foothills of the Highlands, less than an hour from Loch Lomond, two and a half hours from Glencoe.

There is a unity beneath the five great cultural traditions of Scotland though it is more difficult to define than the differences. The Borders, the Celtic Highlands, the Scandinavian influence in the islands and the extreme north-east, the North-East lowlands and the Midlands Belt all relate to one another to make a whole, a community of cousins.

It is a family relationship based partly on familiarity with one another's traditions and habits and partly on contact, each region playing its part in the dramatic tension and interplay of Scottish life. It is founded on the memory of the long history of Scotland as a nation. And even now after two and a half centuries of union with England, Scotland does not forget her heritage.

INDEX OF ILLUSTRATIONS

Bold type indicates a coloured illustration

GENERAL INDEX

For abbeys, battles, castles, glens and lochs see in alphabetical order of second part of name, e.g. Ben An, see An, Ben.